ORIGAMI INSIDE-OUT

Other books by John Montroll:

Origami Sculptures

Origami Sea Life by John Montroll and Robert Lang

Prehistoric Origami *Dinosaurs and Other Creatures*

African Animals in Origami

Animal Origami for the Enthusiast

Origami for the Enthusiast

Easy Origami

ORIGAMI INSIDE-OUT

John Montroll

Dover Publications, Inc.
New York

To Mayo, Naomi, Shelly, Han, Michele, and Alexander

Introduction

Traditional origami focuses on the structure of the folded work of art. Over the last several years, I have been designing projects which combine color patterns with structure. Such designs are possible because standard origami paper is colored on one side and white on the other. My recent book, *African Animals in Origami*, contained several examples of patterned origami, notably the zebra and the giraffe. In this book, I present you with a series of projects where the color patterns are formed by folding inside-out.

Many of these projects also involve the theme of trisection which seems to be creeping into my style more and more. Some examples are the elephant, penguin, Canada goose, and some of the chess pieces.

The book is divided into five sections. The first contains a Martian and few other creatures. The second section details construction of basic geometric shapes, including the tetrahedron, the cube, and the octahedron. The third and fourth sections present a Canada goose, a raccoon, and several other birds and mammals of distinguished coloration. Finally, there is a chessboard and a full set of playing pieces.

Although any square paper can be used for the projects in this book, the best material is standard origami paper. Origami paper is sold in many hobby shops, and it can be purchased by mail from The Friends of the Origami Center of America, 15 West 77 Street, New York, NY 10024-5192. In my diagrams, the shading represents the colored side of the paper. The illustrations conform to the internationally accepted Randlett-Yoshizawa conventions. Large sheets are easier to work with than small ones.

Origami paper, and a catalog of other available craft books, can also be ordered from Dover Publications, Inc., 31 East 2nd St., Mineola, NY 11501.

The directions for each project have been submitted to experienced origami artists, and I thank the many friends whose suggestions have helped me improve the clarity of my illustrations and explanations. I wish to thank my friends Sascha Beiken, Husayn Moody, Matt Dickie, Robert Ross, Tim Getman, Jeremiah Helm, Jon Zeiders, and Paul Gilden from St. Anselm's Abbey School for their descriptions and poems of the models throughout this book.

John Montroll

Contents

* Simple
** Intermediate
*** Complex
**** Very Complex

Creatures

Ghost
*
Page 9

Snowman
**
Page 11

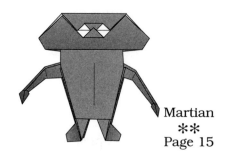

Martian
**
Page 15

Geometrics

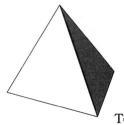

Tetrahedron
*
Page 20

Diamond of Triangles
**
Page 22

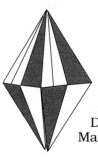

Diamond of
Many Triangles
**
Page 25

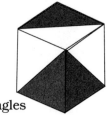

Cube of Triangles
**
Page 28

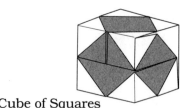

Cube of Squares
**
Page 31

Octahedron
**
Page 34

Birds

Penguin
**
Page 38

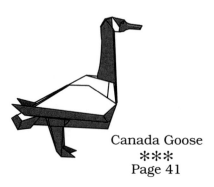

Canada Goose
***
Page 41

Blue Jay
***
Page 47

Mammals

Skunk
✳✳✳
Page 53

Anteater
✳✳✳
Page 58

Raccoon
✳✳✳
Page 64

Tiger
✳✳✳
Page 70

Elephant
✳✳✳
Page 75

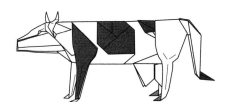

Holstein Cow
✳✳✳✳
Page 83

Chess

Pawn
✳✳
Page 93

Knight
✳✳
Page 96

Bishop
✳✳
Page 98

Rook
✳✳
Page 101

Queen
✳✳
Page 103

King
✳✳
Page 106

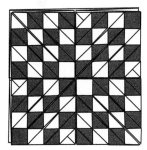

Chess Board & Chess Table
✳✳✳✳
Page 110

Symbols

Lines

— — — — — — — — — — Valley fold, fold in front.

— · · — · — · · — · — · · — Mountain fold, fold behind.

——————————— Crease line.

·· X-ray or guide line.

Arrows

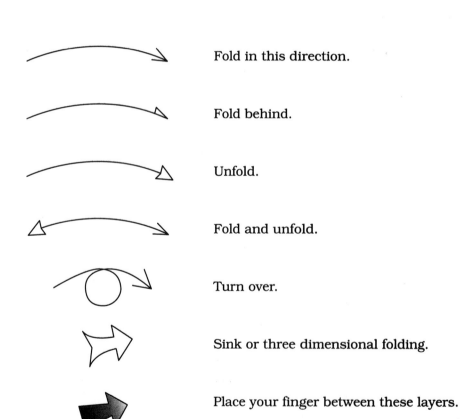

Fold in this direction.

Fold behind.

Unfold.

Fold and unfold.

Turn over.

Sink or three dimensional folding.

Place your finger between these layers.

Ghost

1

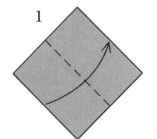

Fold in half.

2

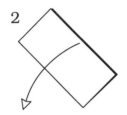

Unfold.

3

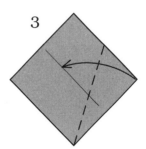

Fold the corner to the center line.

4

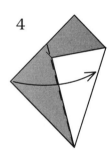

5

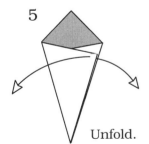

Unfold.

6

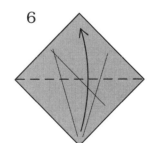

7

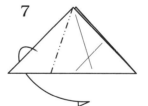

Fold behind along the crease.

8

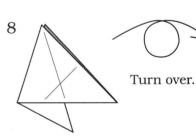

Turn over.

9

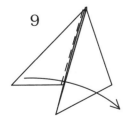

10

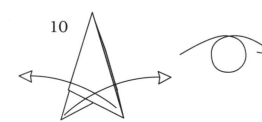

Unfold and turn over.

11

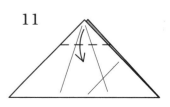

Fold both layers down. There are no guides for this fold.

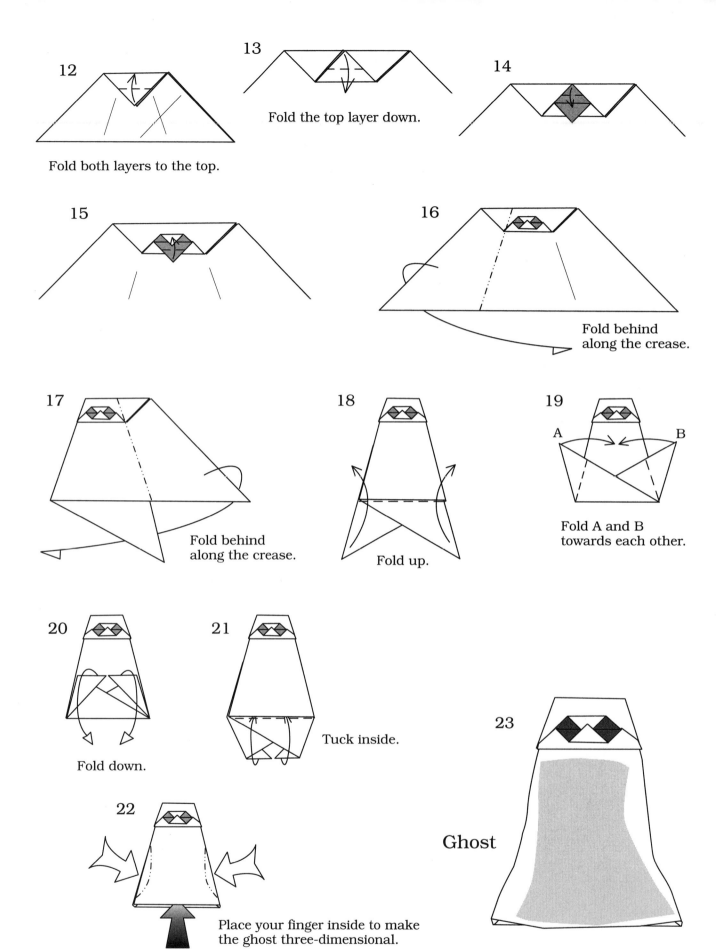

12 Fold both layers to the top.

13 Fold the top layer down.

14

15

16 Fold behind along the crease.

17 Fold behind along the crease.

18 Fold up.

19 Fold A and B towards each other.

20 Fold down.

21 Tuck inside.

22 Place your finger inside to make the ghost three-dimensional.

23 Ghost

Snowman

Ode to a Snowman

The snowman is such a trusty friend;
If it's cold he's in your yard for a week on end.
With his charcoal eyes and his carrot nose,
He only comes 'round when it really snows.
With white snow you build him up from the ground,
Unless of course the dog has been 'round.
He looks so regal ruling your place
'Til Mr. Sun comes about and melts him away.

Tim Getman

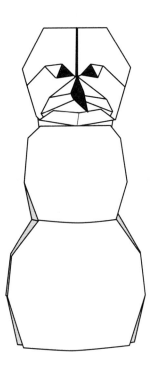

1

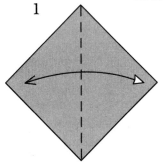

Fold and unfold.

2

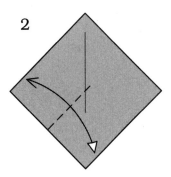

Fold and unfold.

3

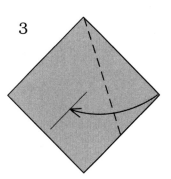

Fold the corner
to the center line.

4

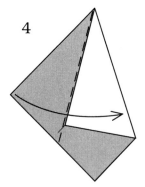

5

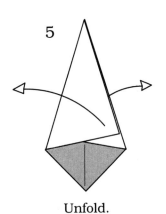

Unfold.

6

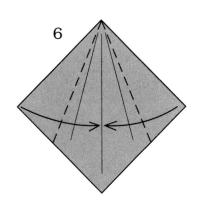

7

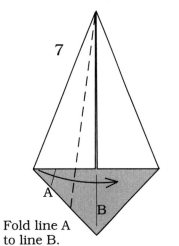

A   B

Fold line A
to line B.

8

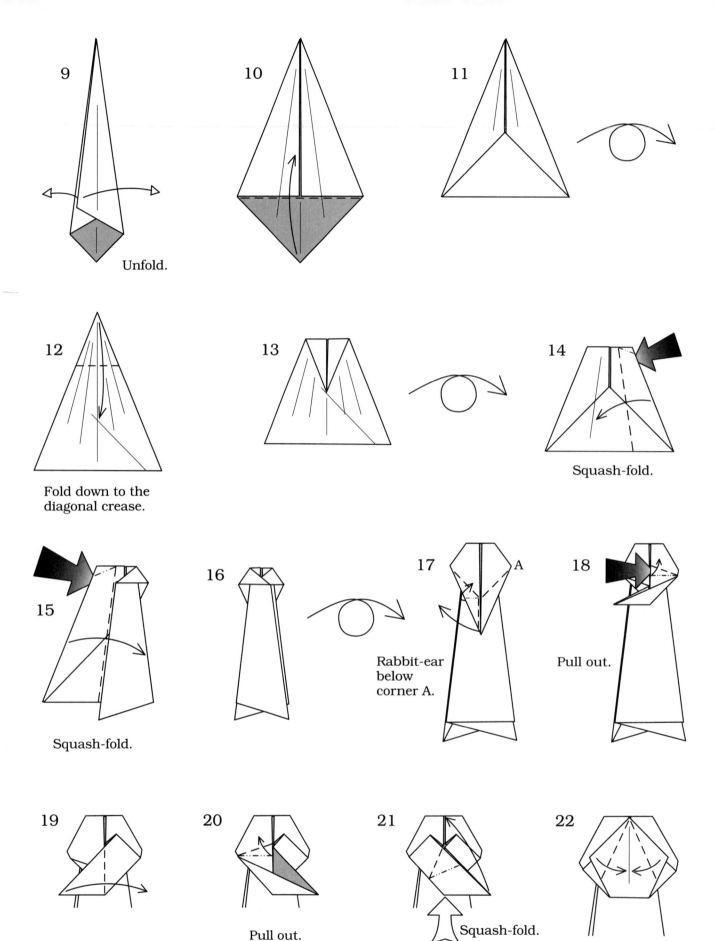

9

Unfold.

10

11

12

Fold down to the
diagonal crease.

13

14

Squash-fold.

15

Squash-fold.

16

17 A

Rabbit-ear
below
corner A.

18

Pull out.

19

20

Pull out.

21

Squash-fold.

22

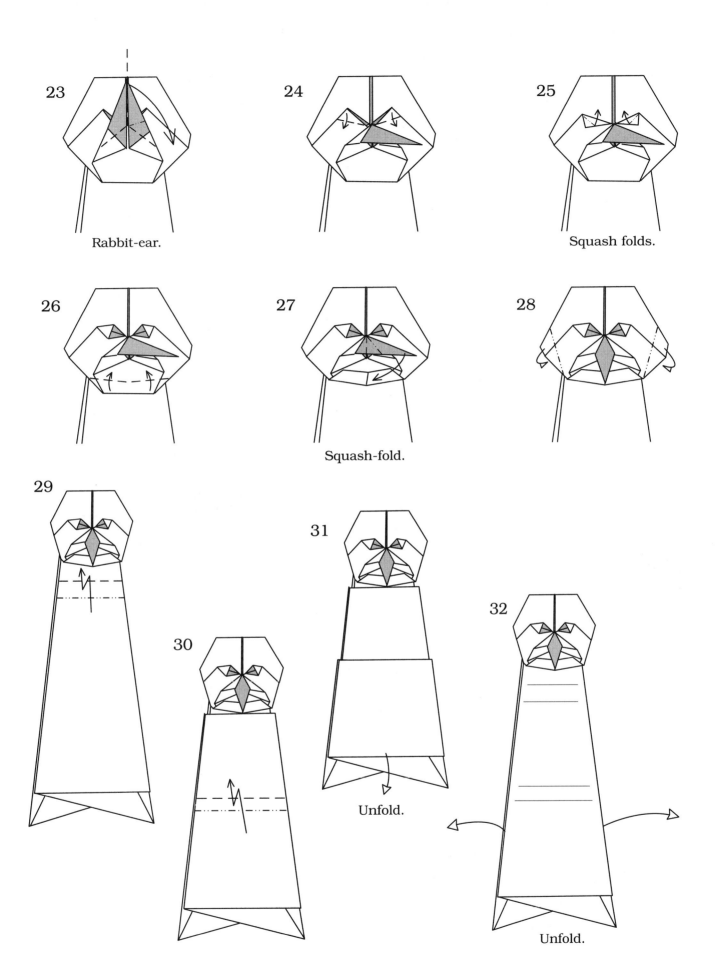

23

Rabbit-ear.

24

25

Squash folds.

26

27

Squash-fold.

28

29

30

31

Unfold.

32

Unfold.

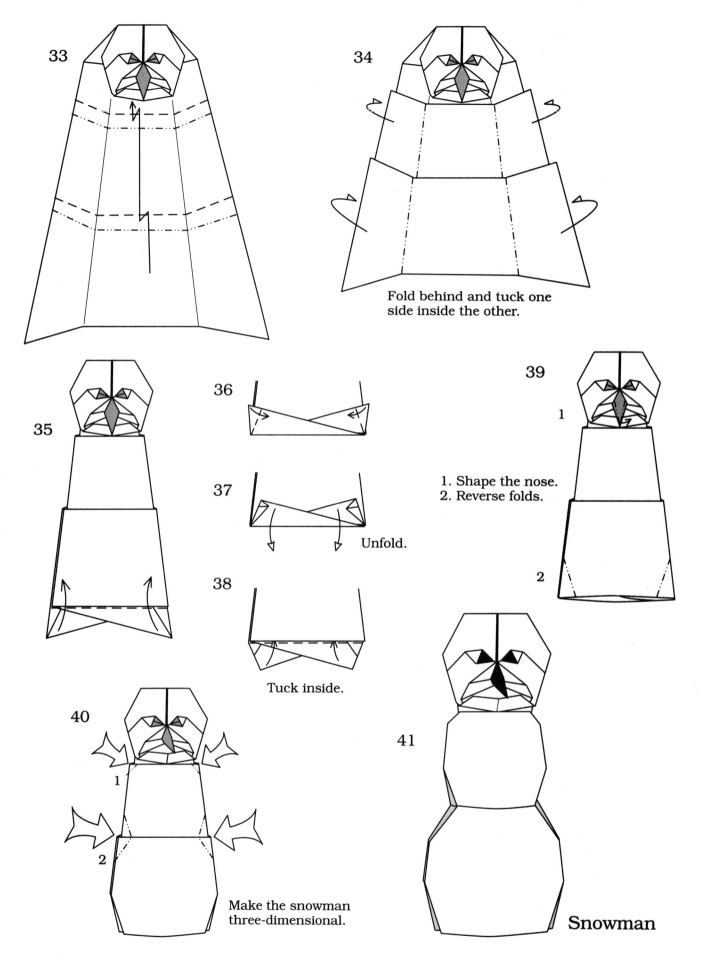

33

34

Fold behind and tuck one side inside the other.

35

36

37 Unfold.

38 Tuck inside.

39

1

2

1. Shape the nose.
2. Reverse folds.

40

1

2

Make the snowman three-dimensional.

41

Snowman

Martian

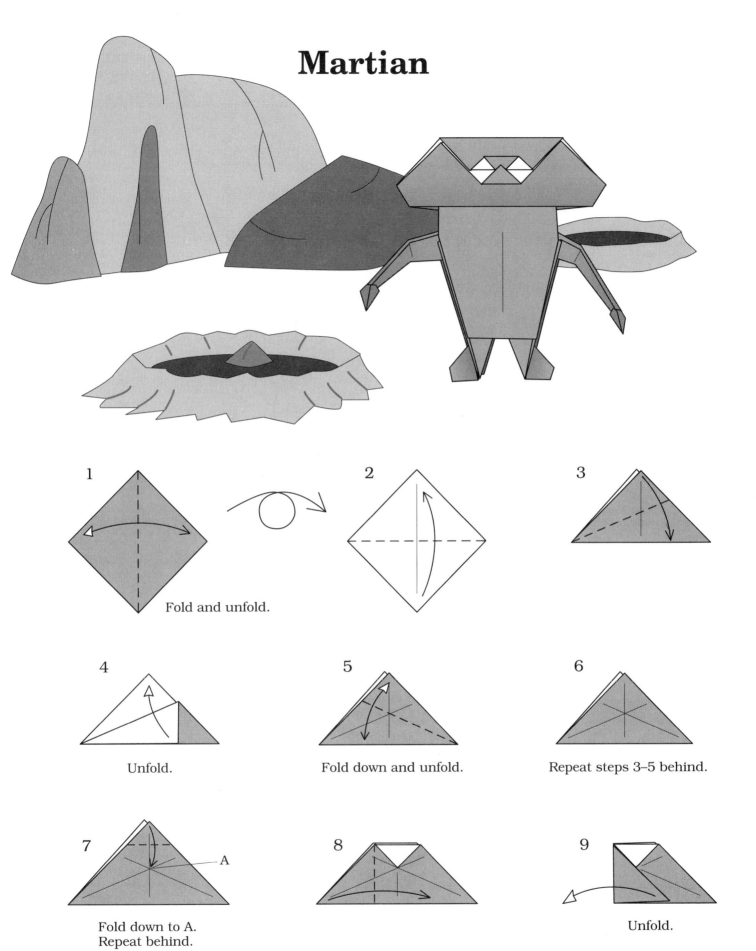

1 Fold and unfold.

2

3

4 Unfold.

5 Fold down and unfold.

6 Repeat steps 3–5 behind.

7 Fold down to A. Repeat behind.

8

9 Unfold.

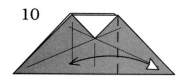

Fold and unfold.

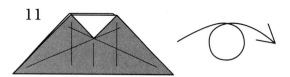

Unfold. Repeat behind.

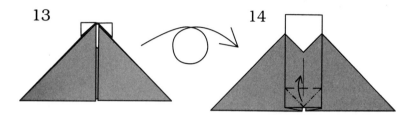

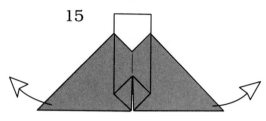

Petal-fold.

Unfold.

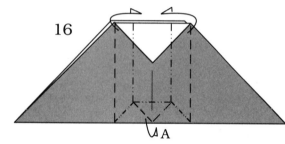

Refold bringing A behind and up.

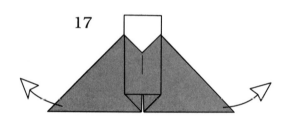

Unfold.

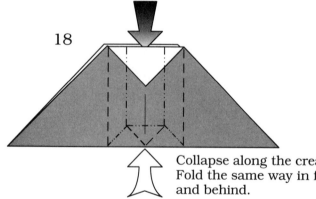

Collapse along the creases.
Fold the same way in front
and behind.

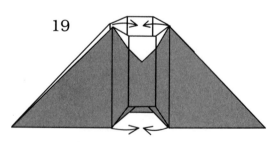

An intermediate
three-dimensional step.

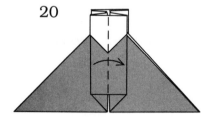

Repeat behind.

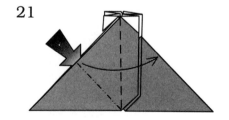

Squash-fold. Repeat behind.

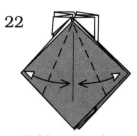

Fold and unfold.

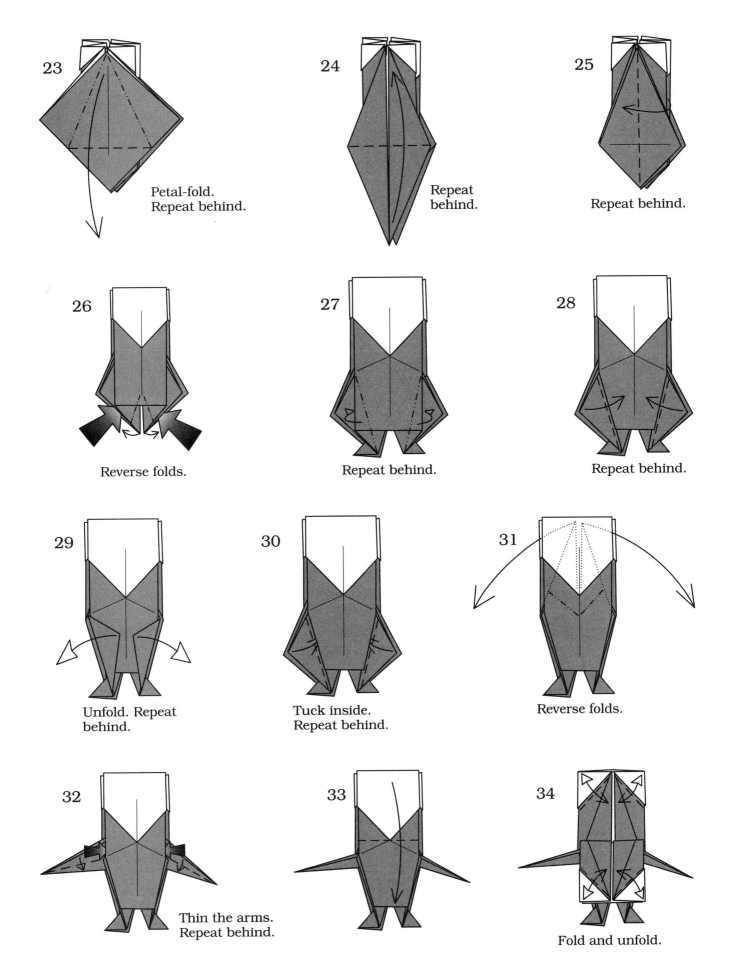

23 Petal-fold.
Repeat behind.

24 Repeat behind.

25 Repeat behind.

26 Reverse folds.

27 Repeat behind.

28 Repeat behind.

29 Unfold. Repeat behind.

30 Tuck inside.
Repeat behind.

31 Reverse folds.

32 Thin the arms.
Repeat behind.

33

34 Fold and unfold.

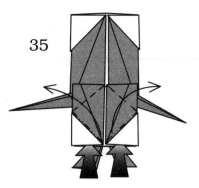

35

Corner A—see the next step—will come out while making these squash folds.

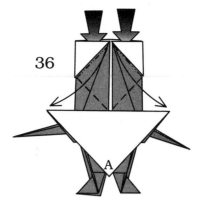

36

Squash folds.

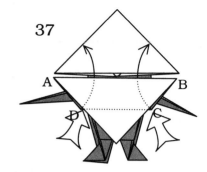

37

Fold region ABCD inside-out.

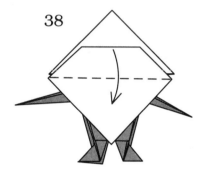

38

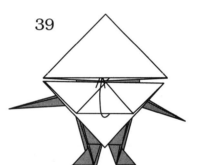

39

Tuck inside.

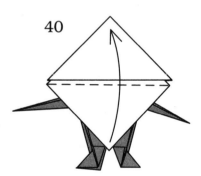

40

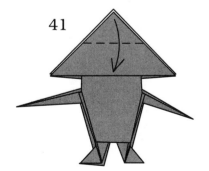

41

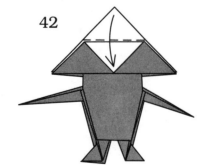

42

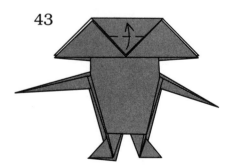

43

44

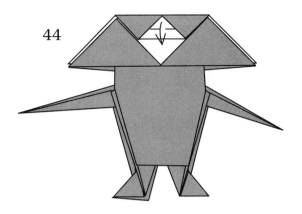

45

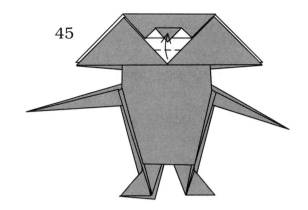

46

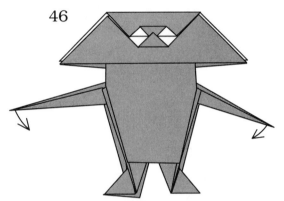

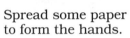

Spread some paper
to form the hands.

47

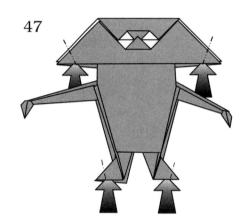

Four reverse folds.

48

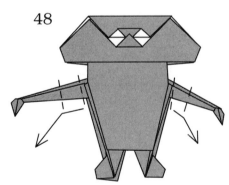

Bend the arms. Adjust the
feet so the Martian can stand.

49

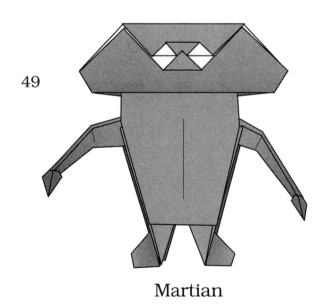

Martian

Geometrics

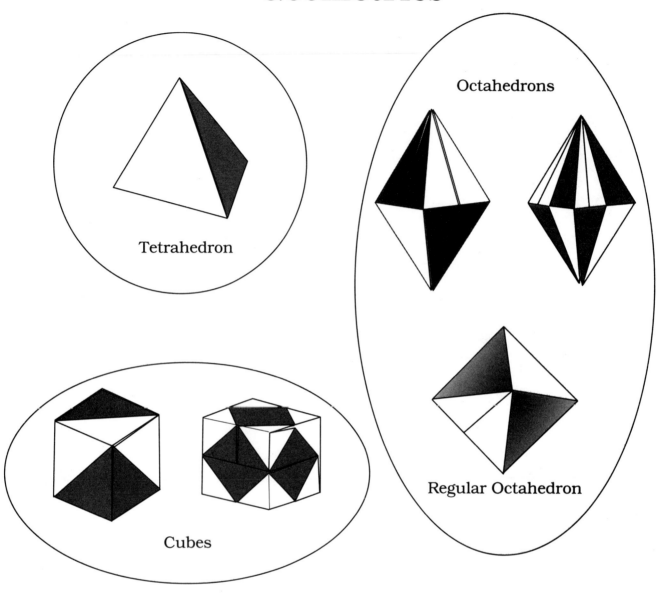

Tetrahedron

Octahedrons

Regular Octahedron

Cubes

Tetrahedron

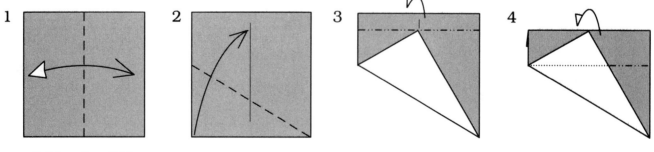

1   2   3   4

Fold and unfold.

5

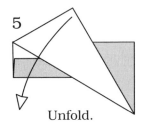

Unfold.

6

7

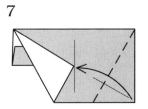

8

9

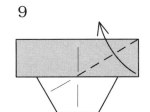

10

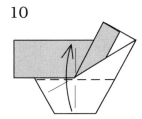

11

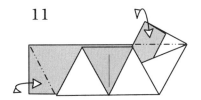

Fold behind and unfold.

12

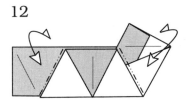

Fold behind and unfold.

13

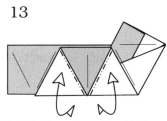

Fold behind and unfold.

14

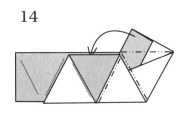

Tuck inside.

15

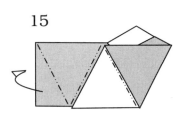

Wrap around and
tuck inside.

16

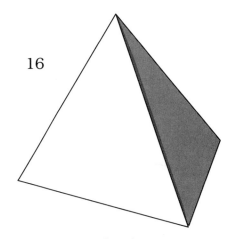

Tetrahedron

Diamond of Triangles

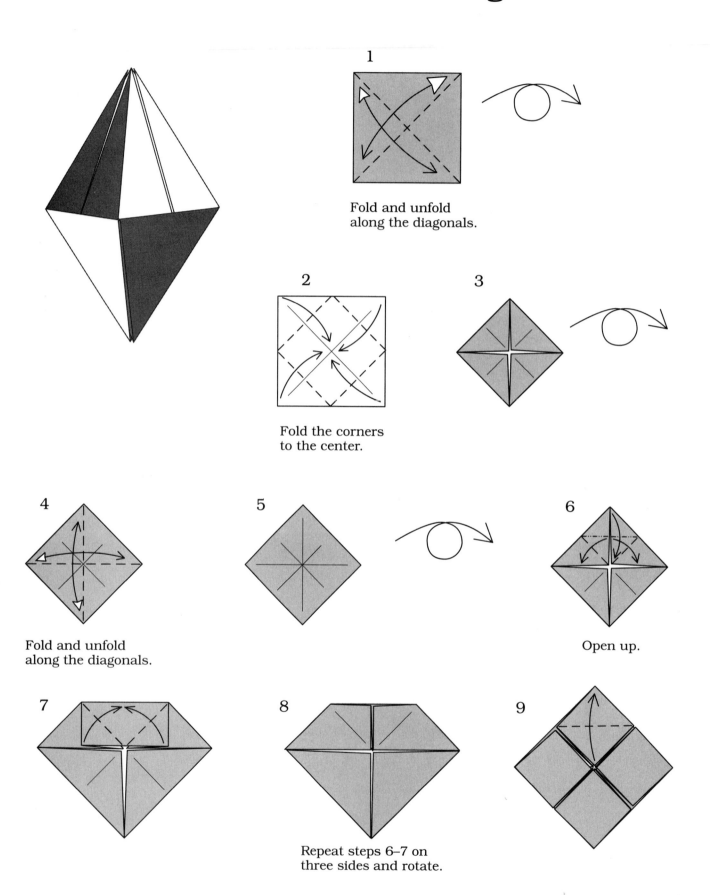

1

Fold and unfold
along the diagonals.

2

Fold the corners
to the center.

3

4

Fold and unfold
along the diagonals.

5

6

Open up.

7

8

Repeat steps 6–7 on
three sides and rotate.

9

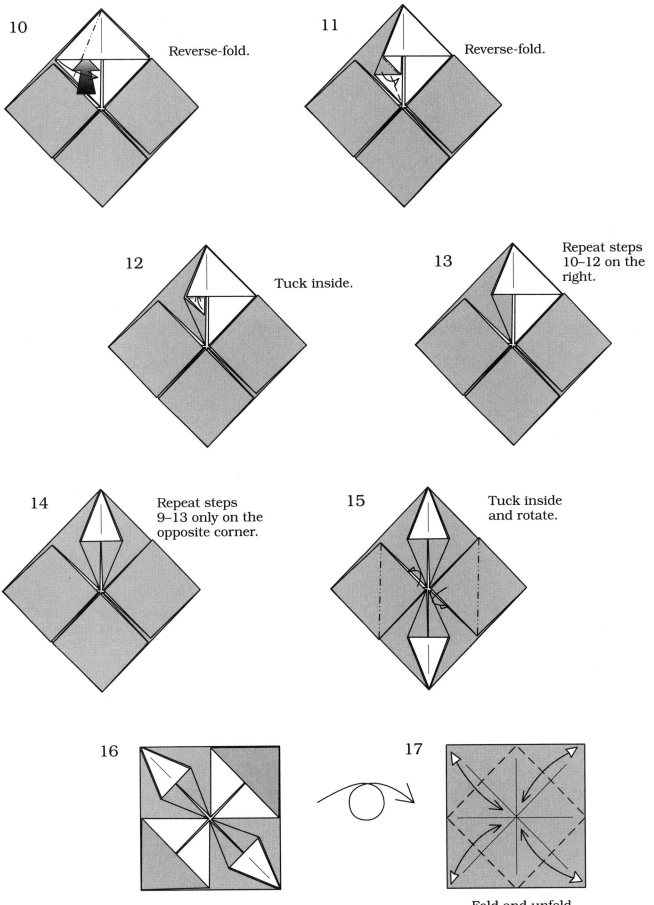

10   Reverse-fold.

11   Reverse-fold.

12   Tuck inside.

13   Repeat steps 10–12 on the right.

14   Repeat steps 9–13 only on the opposite corner.

15   Tuck inside and rotate.

16

17   Fold and unfold.

18

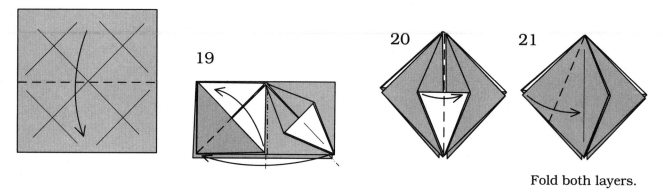

19

20

21

Fold both layers.

22

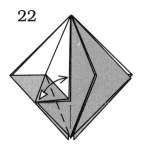

Fold and unfold.

23

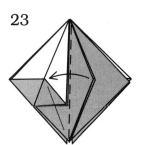

24

Repeat steps 20–23 on
the right and behind.

25

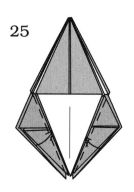

Tuck inside,
repeat behind.

26

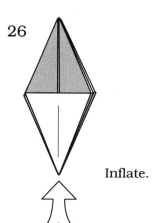

Inflate.

27

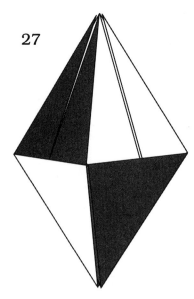

Diamond of Triangles

Diamond of Many Triangles

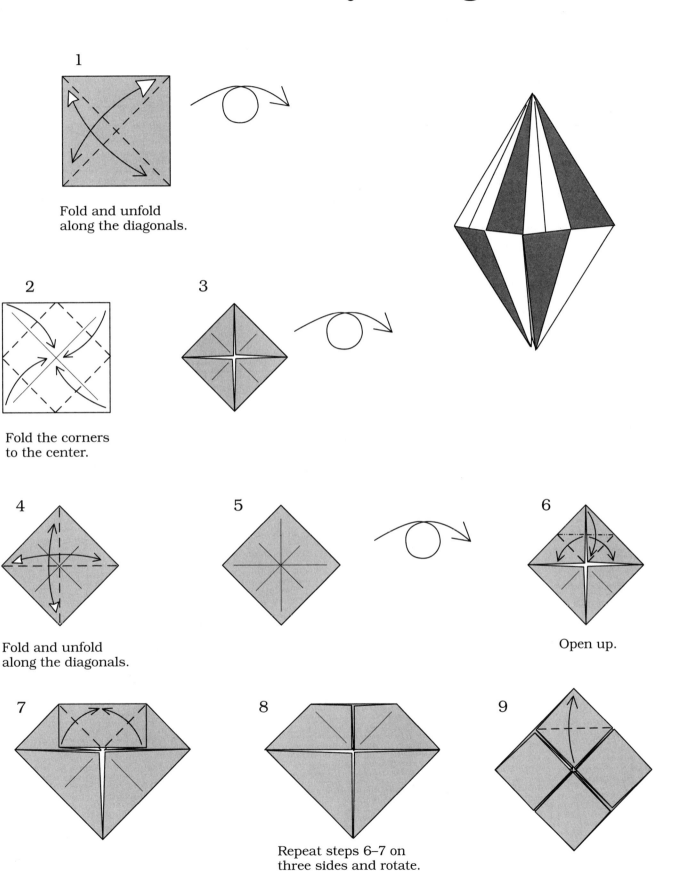

1

Fold and unfold
along the diagonals.

2

Fold the corners
to the center.

3

4

Fold and unfold
along the diagonals.

5

6

Open up.

7

8

Repeat steps 6–7 on
three sides and rotate.

9

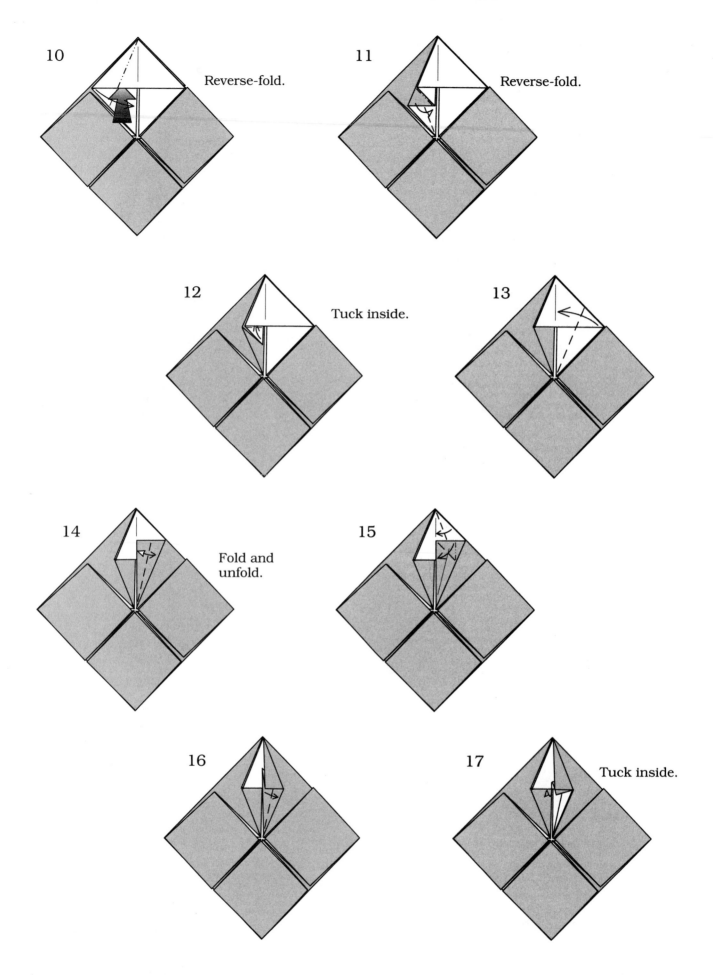

10   Reverse-fold.

11   Reverse-fold.

12   Tuck inside.

13

14   Fold and unfold.

15

16

17   Tuck inside.

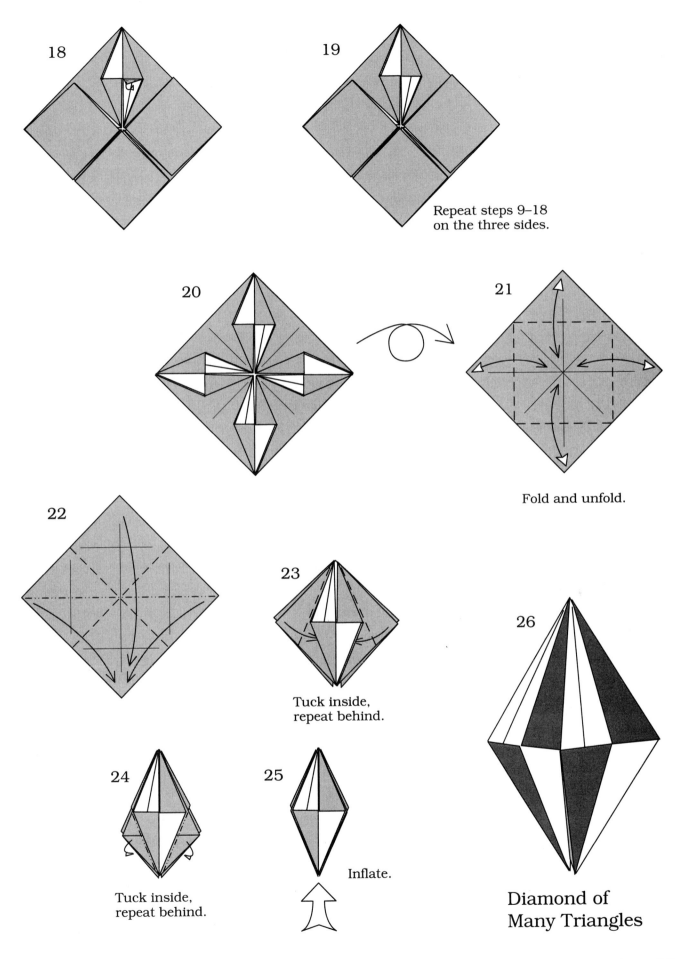

18

19

Repeat steps 9–18
on the three sides.

20

21

Fold and unfold.

22

23

Tuck inside,
repeat behind.

24

Tuck inside,
repeat behind.

25

Inflate.

26

Diamond of
Many Triangles

Diamond of Many Triangles **27**

Cube of Triangles

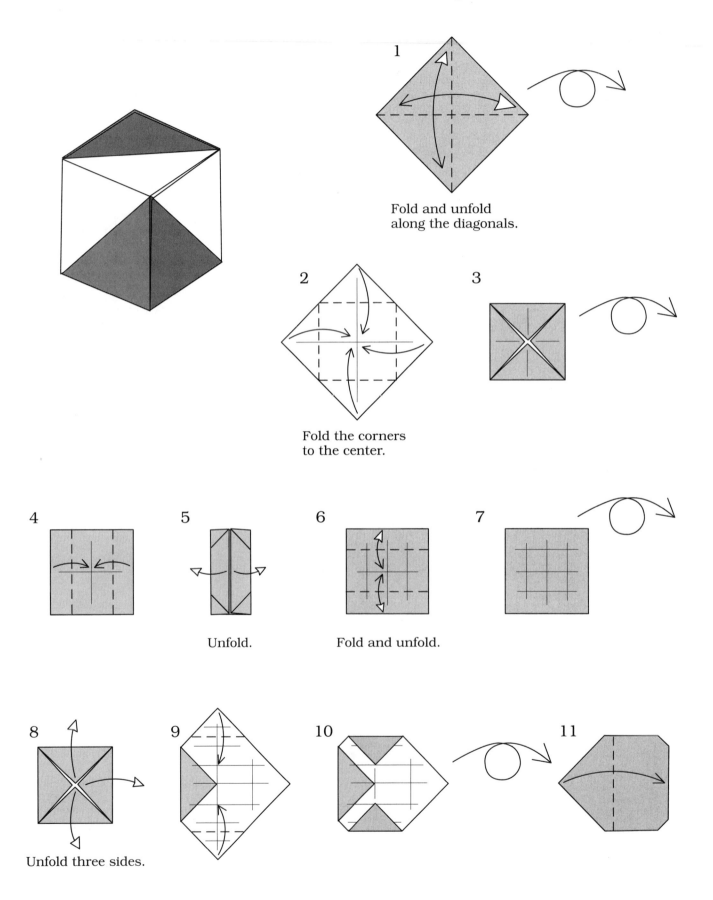

1 Fold and unfold along the diagonals.

2 Fold the corners to the center.

3

4

5 Unfold.

6 Fold and unfold.

7

8 Unfold three sides.

9

10

11

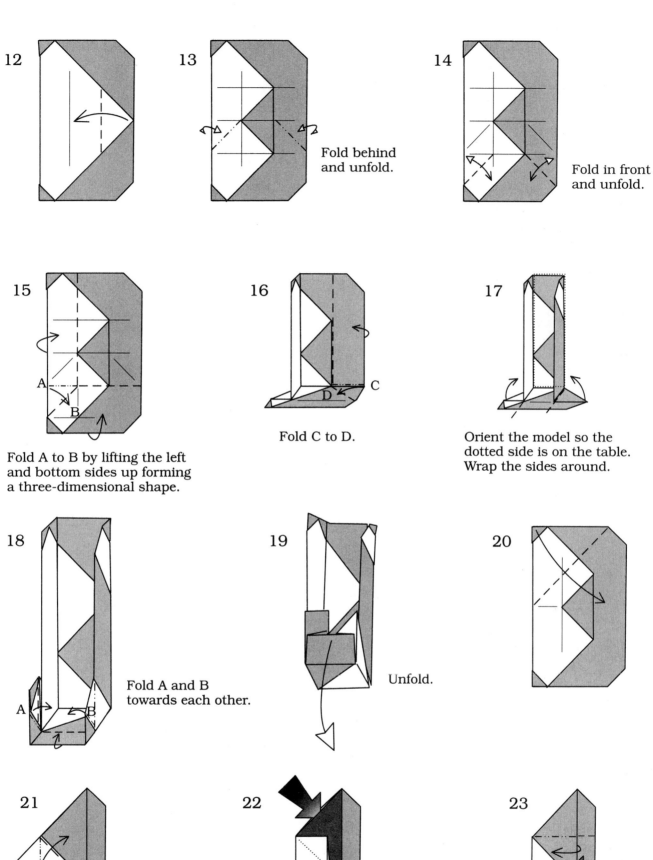

12

13 Fold behind and unfold.

14 Fold in front and unfold.

15 Fold A to B by lifting the left and bottom sides up forming a three-dimensional shape.

16 Fold C to D.

17 Orient the model so the dotted side is on the table. Wrap the sides around.

18 Fold A and B towards each other.

19 Unfold.

20

21 Squash-fold.

22 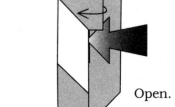 Place the dark paper on top.

23 Open.

24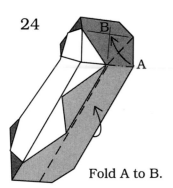

Fold A to B.

25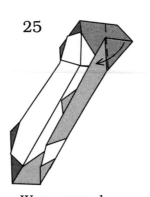

Wrap around.

26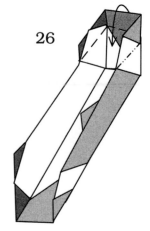

Fold in on all
three sides.

27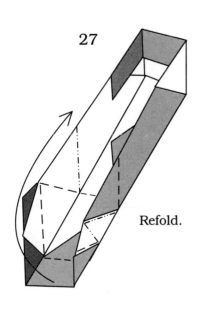

Refold.

28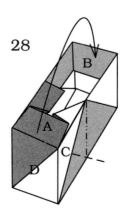

Bring A to B. Sides A and
C will be tucked inside so
side D will become the top.

29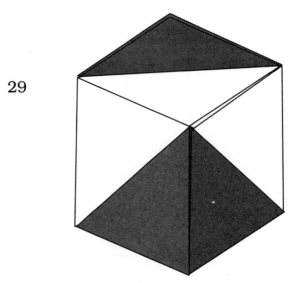

Cube of Triangles

Cube of Squares

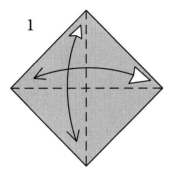

1

Fold and unfold
along the diagonals.

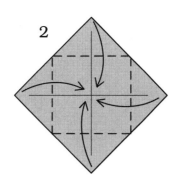

2

Fold the corners
to the center.

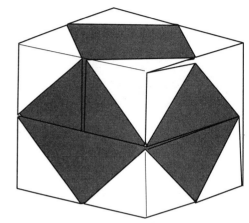

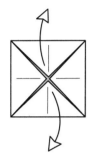

3

Unfold.

4

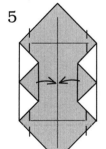

5

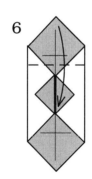

6

7

Unfold.

8

Unfold.

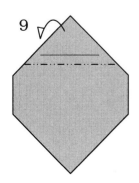

9

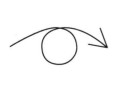

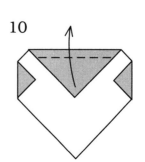

10

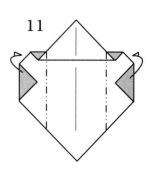

11

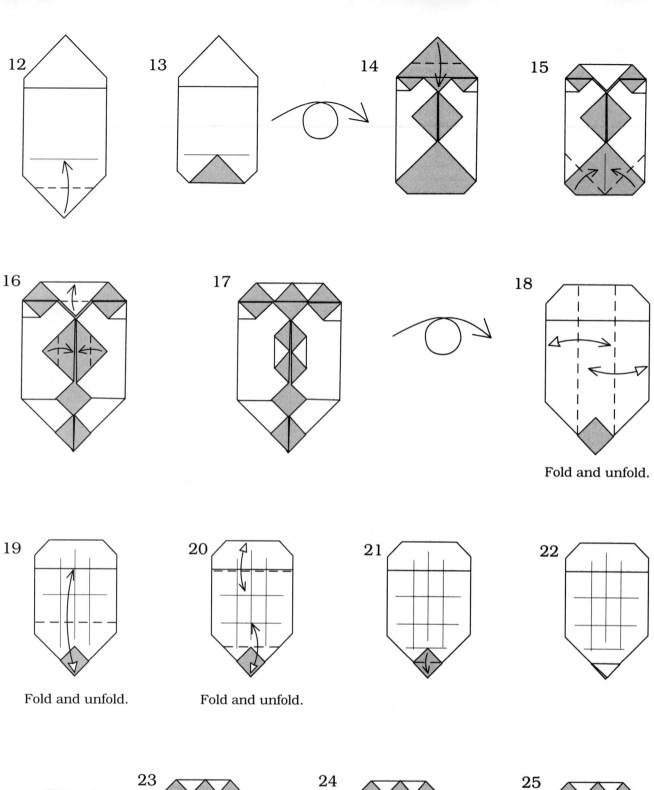

12

13

14

15

16

17

18

Fold and unfold.

19

Fold and unfold.

20

Fold and unfold.

21

22

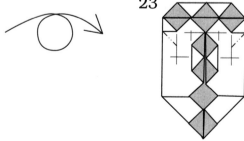

23

Fold and unfold.

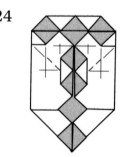

24

Fold and unfold.

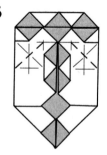

25

Fold and unfold.

26

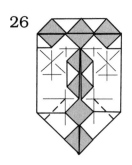

Fold and unfold.

27

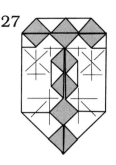

Turn over and rotate.

28

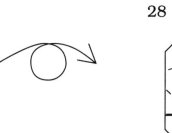

29

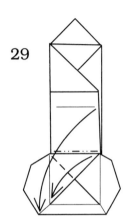

Repeat on
the right.

30

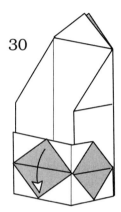

Unfold.

31

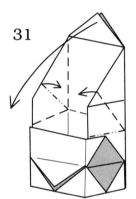

32

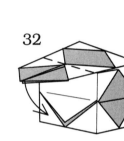

33

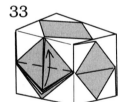

Fold two layers up.

34

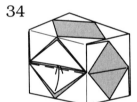

Tuck inside.

35

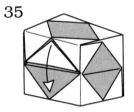

Unfold one layer.

36

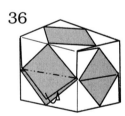

Fold behind the
lower layer.

37

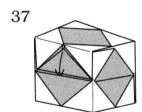

Tuck inside.

38

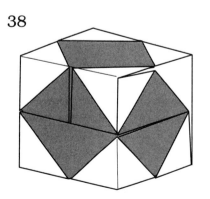

Cube of Squares

Octahedron

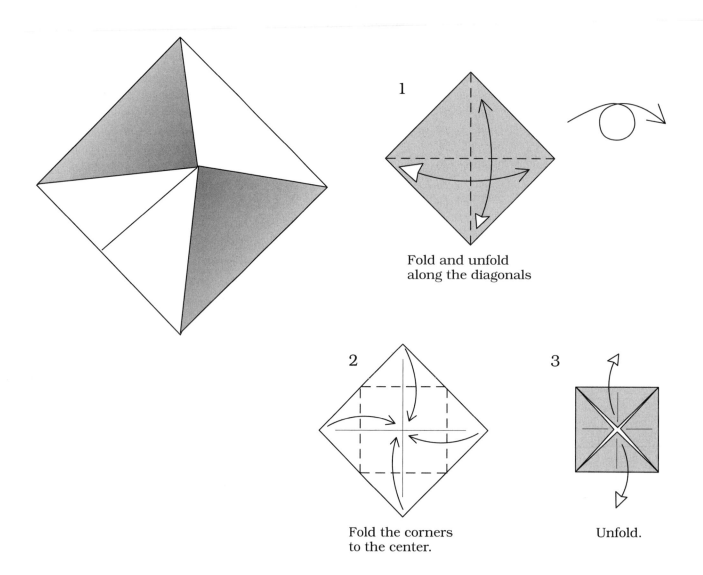

1

Fold and unfold
along the diagonals

2

Fold the corners
to the center.

3

Unfold.

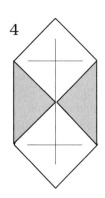

4

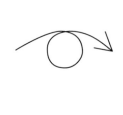

5

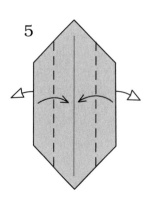

6

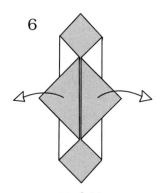

Unfold.

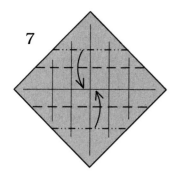

7

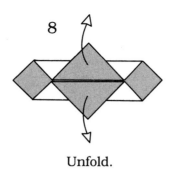

8

Unfold.

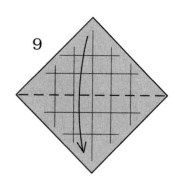

9

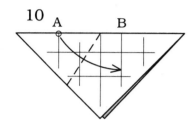

10

A   B

Fold point A to line B.

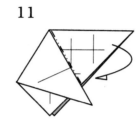

11

12

Repeat behind.

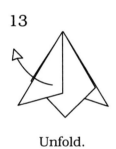

13

Unfold.

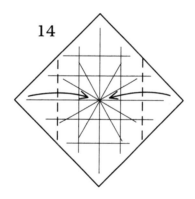

14

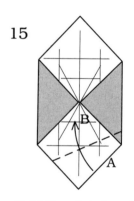

15

B

A

Fold line A to line B.

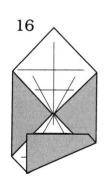

16

17

Fold up and unfold
along the crease.

18

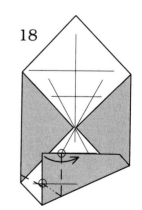

Squash-fold.

19

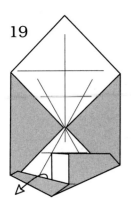

Unfold.

20

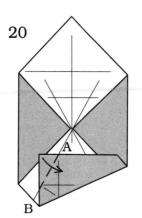

A

B

Fold along line A–B.

21

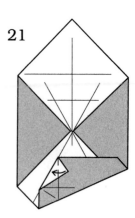

22

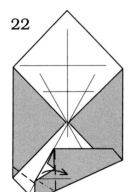

Squash-fold.

23

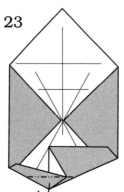

24

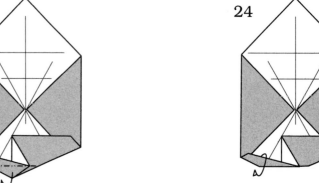

25

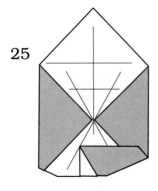

Rotate.

26

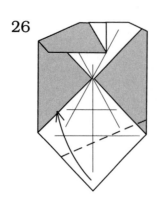

Repeat steps 15–24.

27

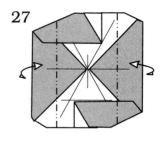

28

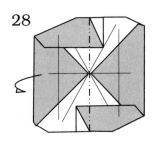

Rotate.

29

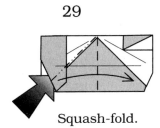

Squash-fold.

30

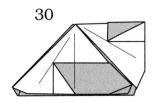

31

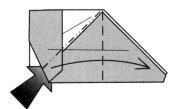

Squash-fold.

32

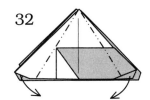

Reverse-folds,
repeat behind.

33

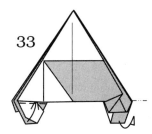

Tuck inside,
repeat behind.

34

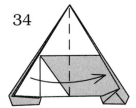

Repeat behind.

35

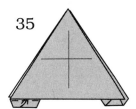

Tuck inside, repeat behind.

36

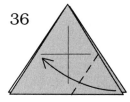

Repeat behind.

37

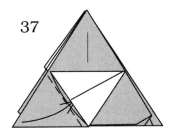

Tuck inside, repeat behind.

38

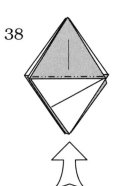

Blow into the bottom.

39

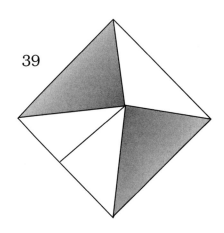

Octahedron

Penguin

The penguin is an unusual bird that stands upright on very short legs and waddles in a clumsy but amusing fashion. Though penguins cannot fly, they are superb swimmers. Penguins live in the southern hemisphere of the world. Many kinds live on the glaciers of the Antarctic, while others are located farther north in regions touched by cold sea currents that originate in Antarctica. Penguin colonies can be found in New Zealand, Australia, and South Africa, as well as the Galapogos Islands. They are not present in any other parts of the world due to the fact that they will not cross into warm ocean currents from the freezing waters of the Antarctic.

All penguins have short, thick feathers on their hefty bodies. Their feathers are white on the belly and black or a bluish color on the back. Some penguins have crests of long feathers and blotches of brightly colored feathers on their short, stocky necks. They have a waterproof coat composed of short, thick feathers and layers of blubber. This allows them to keep warm in their extremely cold climate.

Penguins thrive on fish, and they spend most of their time in water. However, they lay their eggs and raise their young on land. While on land, they make their enormous nests in huge colonies called rookeries. A single rookery can contain up to one million birds. Most of the species make their nests on bare ground or in the grass. Some penguins lay their eggs in shallow holes scraped in the dirt, while a few species lay their eggs in tunnels dug in the ground.

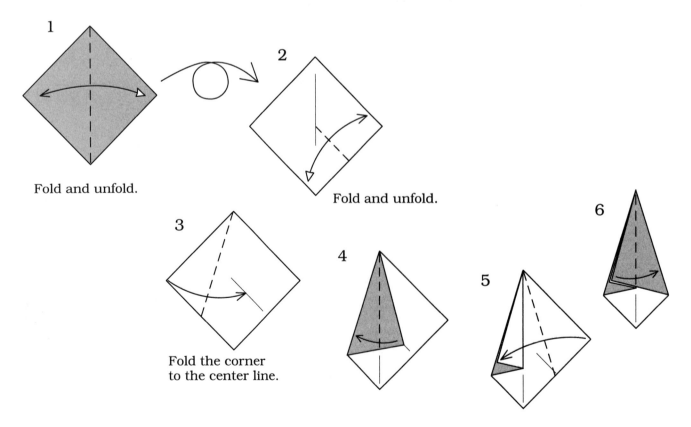

1

Fold and unfold.

2

Fold and unfold.

3

Fold the corner to the center line.

4

5

6

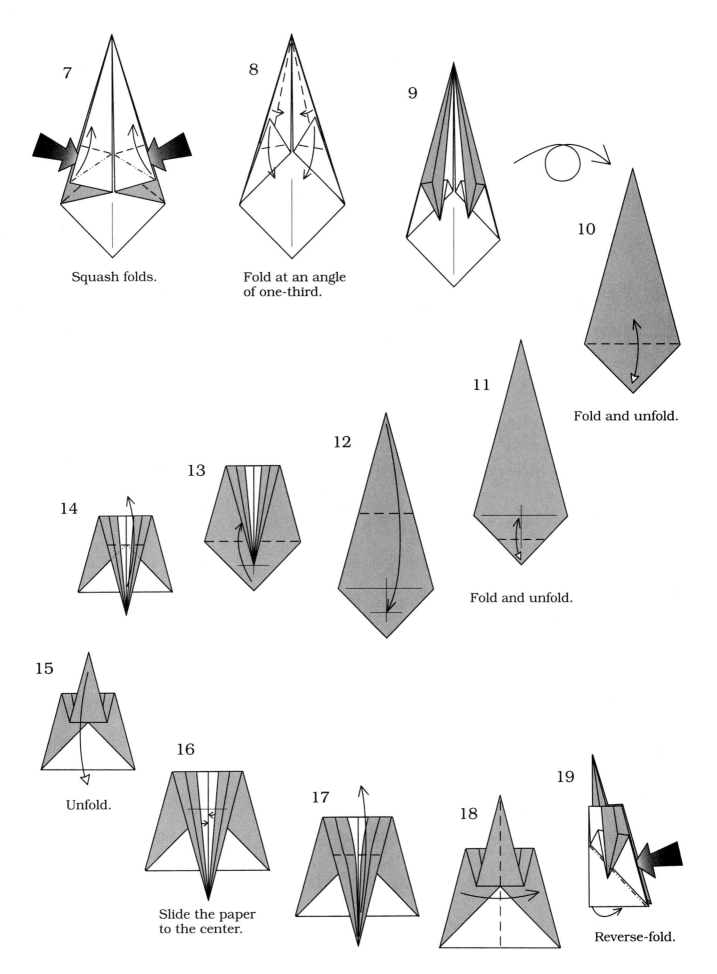

7

Squash folds.

8

Fold at an angle
of one-third.

9

10

Fold and unfold.

11

12

Fold and unfold.

13

14

15

Unfold.

16

Slide the paper
to the center.

17

18

19

Reverse-fold.

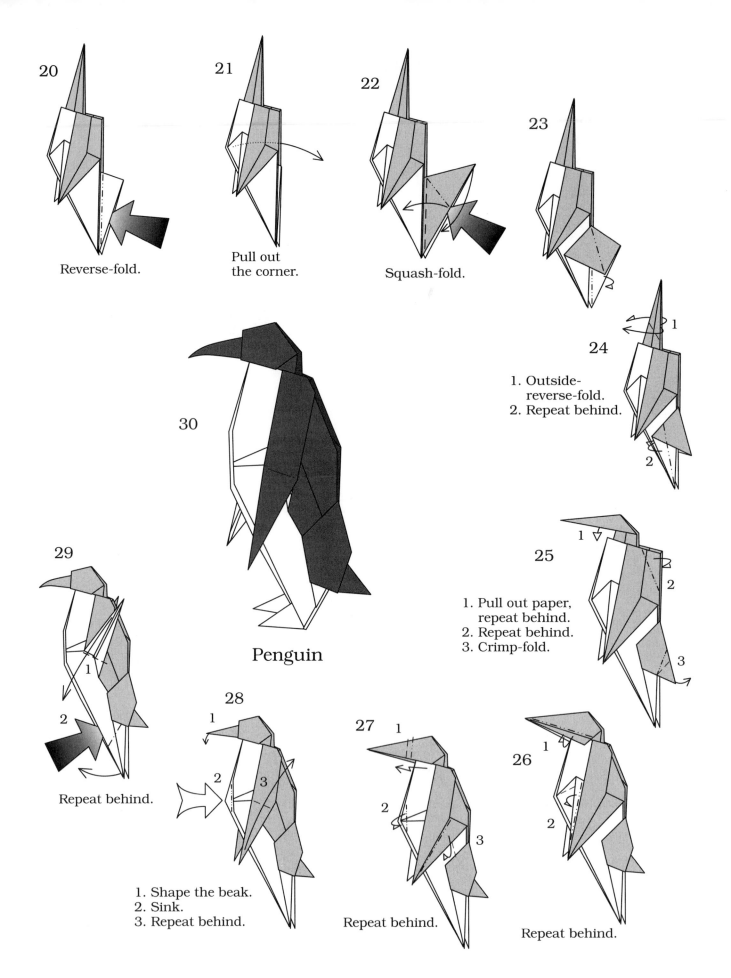

20

Reverse-fold.

21

Pull out
the corner.

22

Squash-fold.

23

24

1. Outside-
   reverse-fold.
2. Repeat behind.

25

1. Pull out paper,
   repeat behind.
2. Repeat behind.
3. Crimp-fold.

26

Repeat behind.

27

Repeat behind.

28

1. Shape the beak.
2. Sink.
3. Repeat behind.

29

Repeat behind.

30

Penguin

Canada Goose

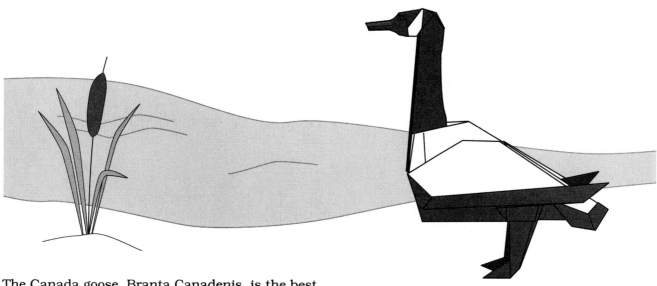

The Canada goose, Branta Canadenis, is the best known goose in North America. It is recognized by the white band across its throat and cheeks. The bird is more often found on land than other waterfowl because of its love for seeds and grains. The long neck is well adapted for grazing. Canada geese migrate in their famous V formations, honking nosily as they fly.

1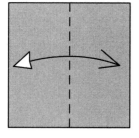

Fold and unfold.

2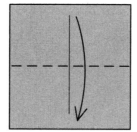

3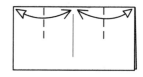

Fold to the center and unfold, creasing only the top half.

4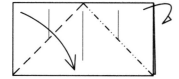

5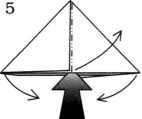

6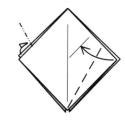

Fold to the crease, repeat at the opposite side.

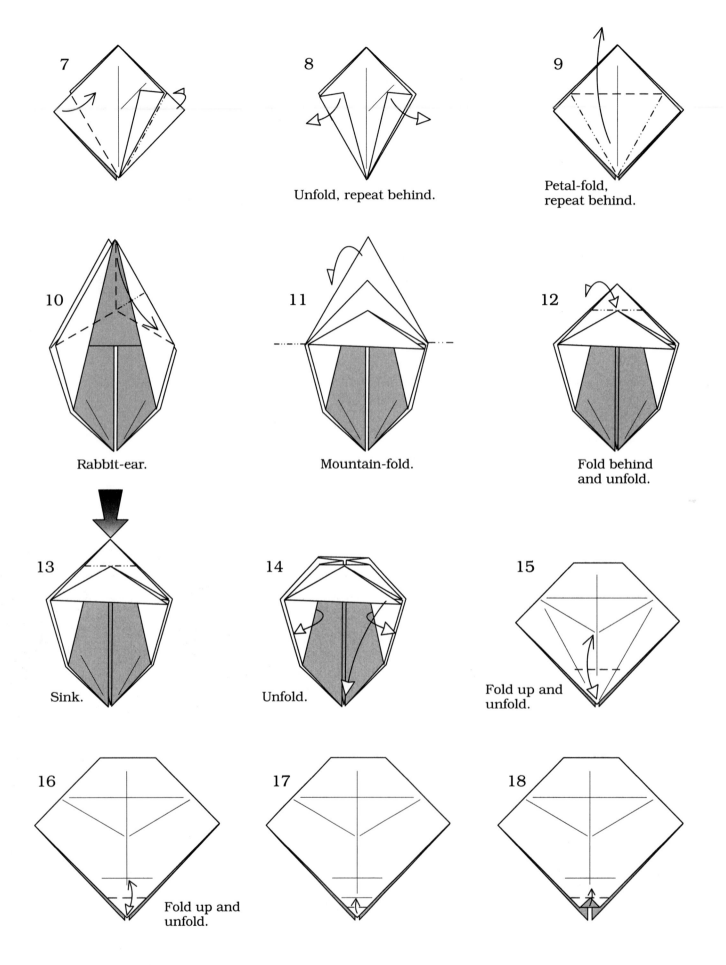

7

8

Unfold, repeat behind.

9

Petal-fold,
repeat behind.

10

Rabbit-ear.

11

Mountain-fold.

12

Fold behind
and unfold.

13

Sink.

14

Unfold.

15

Fold up and
unfold.

16

Fold up and
unfold.

17

18

19

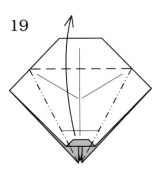

Petal-fold,
repeat behind.

20

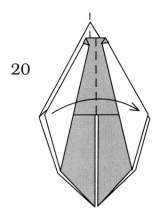

Repeat behind.

21

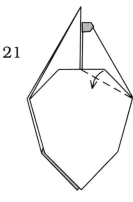

Repeat behind.

22

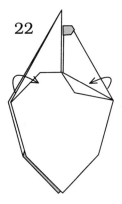

Fold inside-out,
repeat behind.

23

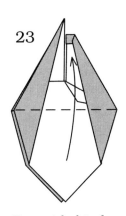

Repeat behind.

24

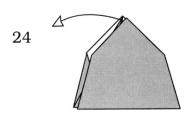

Pull out.

25

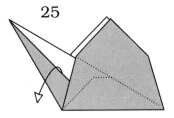

Pull out, repeat behind.

26

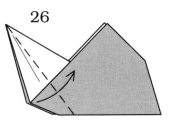

Repeat behind.

27

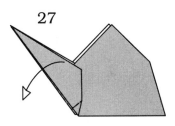

Unfold, repeat behind.

28

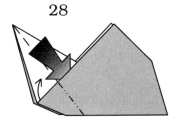

Reverse-fold, repeat behind.

29

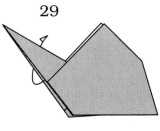

Open.

30

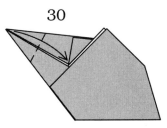

This is three-dimensional,
do not flatten it.

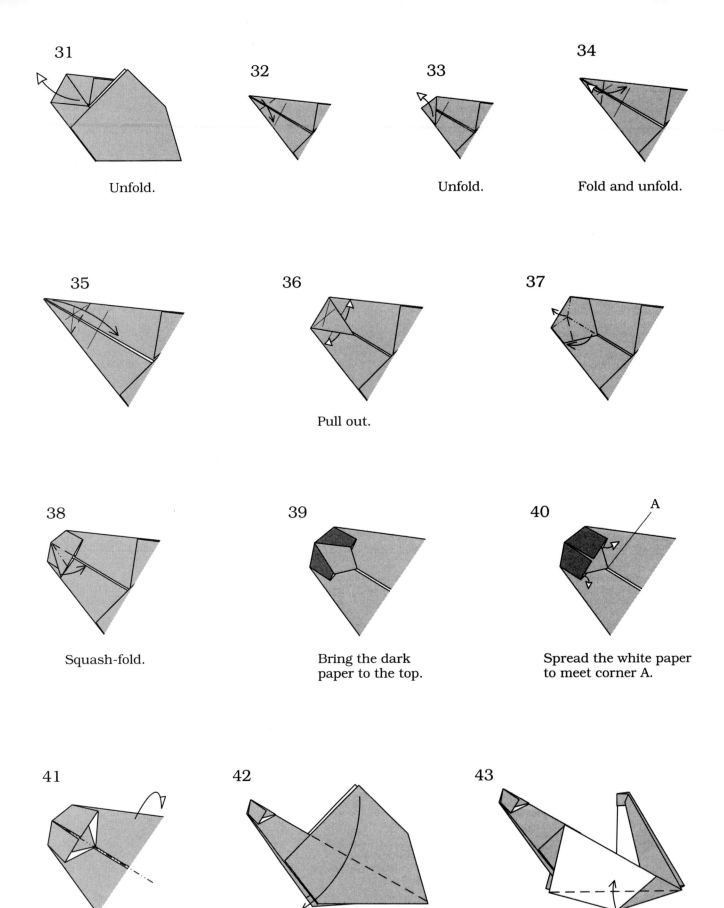

31

Unfold.

32

33

Unfold.

34

Fold and unfold.

35

36

Pull out.

37

38

Squash-fold.

39

Bring the dark
paper to the top.

40

A

Spread the white paper
to meet corner A.

41

42

Repeat behind.

43

Repeat behind.

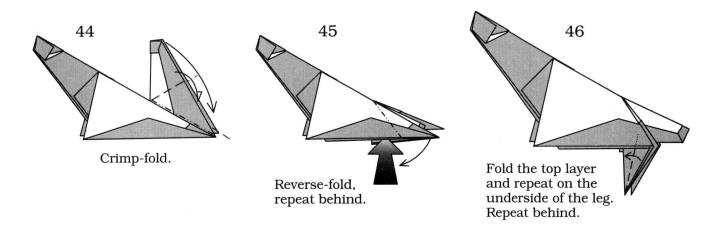

44

Crimp-fold.

45

Reverse-fold, repeat behind.

46

Fold the top layer and repeat on the underside of the leg. Repeat behind.

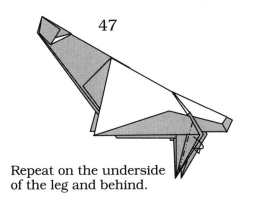

47

Repeat on the underside of the leg and behind.

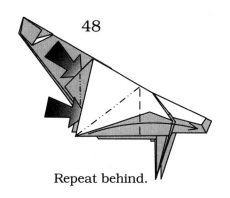

48

Repeat behind.

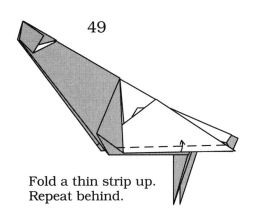

49

Fold a thin strip up. Repeat behind.

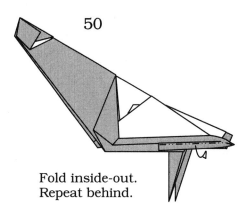

50

Fold inside-out. Repeat behind.

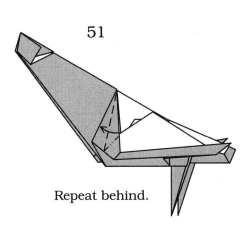

51

Repeat behind.

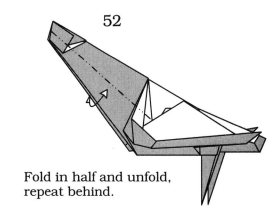

52

Fold in half and unfold, repeat behind.

Canada Goose 45

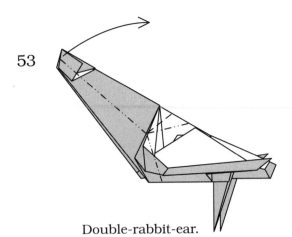

53

Double-rabbit-ear.

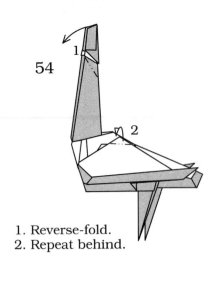

54

1. Reverse-fold.
2. Repeat behind.

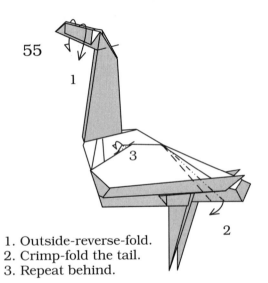

55

1. Outside-reverse-fold.
2. Crimp-fold the tail.
3. Repeat behind.

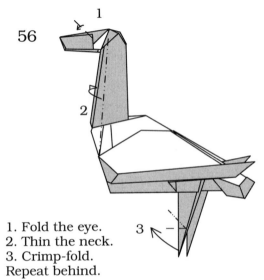

56

1. Fold the eye.
2. Thin the neck.
3. Crimp-fold.
Repeat behind.

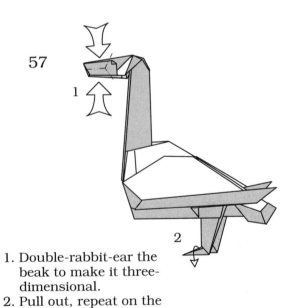

57

1. Double-rabbit-ear the beak to make it three-dimensional.
2. Pull out, repeat on the other side of the foot, repeat behind.

58

Canada Goose

Blue Jay

The blue jay is one of the most common birds in North America, and its bright blue color and distinctive crest make it one of the easiest to identify. Blue jays thrive in populated areas. They are frequent visitors to bird feeders, often driving off smaller birds with harsh warning calls.

1

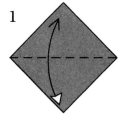

Fold and unfold.

2

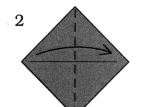

3

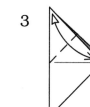

Fold and unfold, creasing lightly.

4

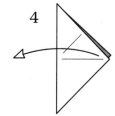

5

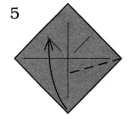

Fold the corner to the crease line. Crease on the right side.

6

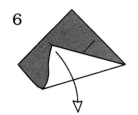

7

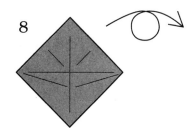

Fold up and unfold.

8

Turn over and rotate.

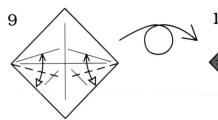

9

Fold up to the crease
line and unfold.

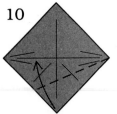

10

Crease lightly.

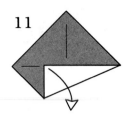

11

Unfold.

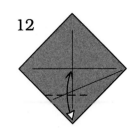

12

Fold up to the center
and unfold. Crease
lightly and only on
the left side.

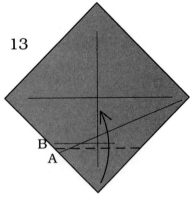

13

Fold up so that A meets the
line above it, close to B.

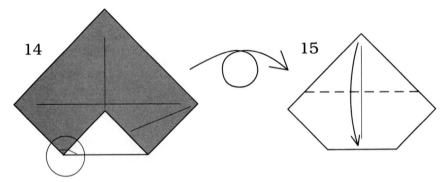

14

Note how the creases
intersect inside the circle.

15

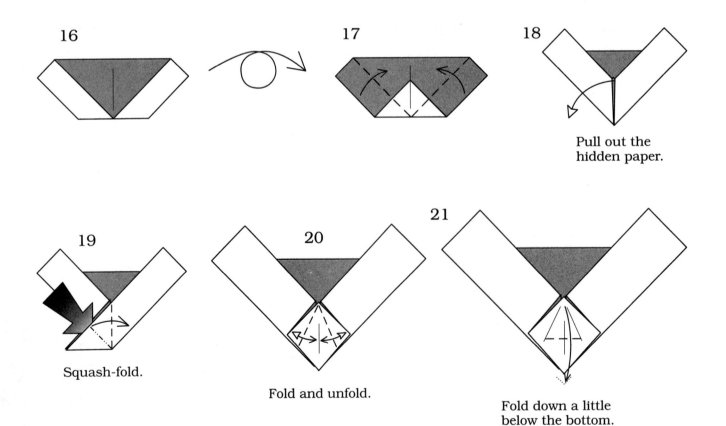

16

17

18

Pull out the
hidden paper.

19

Squash-fold.

20

Fold and unfold.

21

Fold down a little
below the bottom.

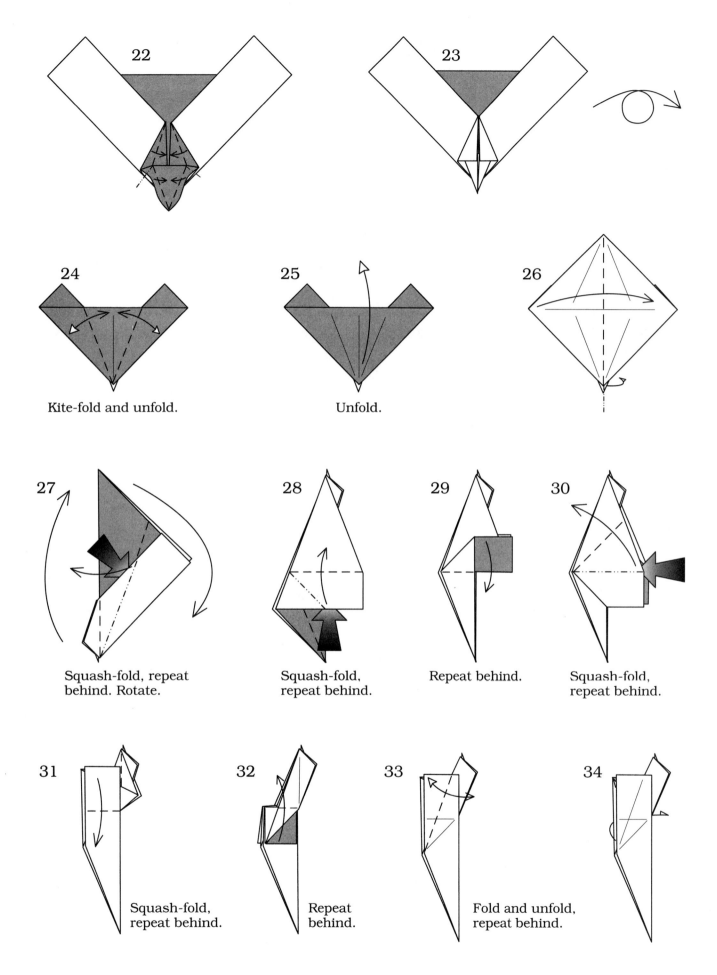

22

23

24

Kite-fold and unfold.

25

Unfold.

26

27

Squash-fold, repeat
behind. Rotate.

28

Squash-fold,
repeat behind.

29

Repeat behind.

30

Squash-fold,
repeat behind.

31

Squash-fold,
repeat behind.

32

Repeat
behind.

33

Fold and unfold,
repeat behind.

34

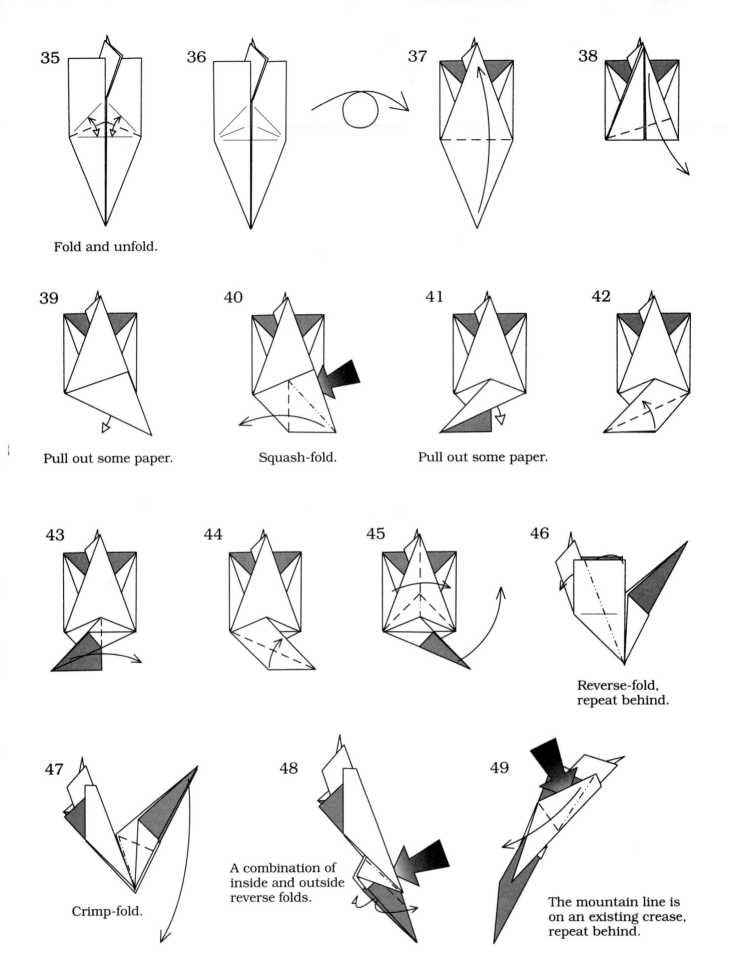

35 Fold and unfold.

36

37

38

39 Pull out some paper.

40 Squash-fold.

41 Pull out some paper.

42

43

44

45

46 Reverse-fold, repeat behind.

47 Crimp-fold.

48 A combination of inside and outside reverse folds.

49 The mountain line is on an existing crease, repeat behind.

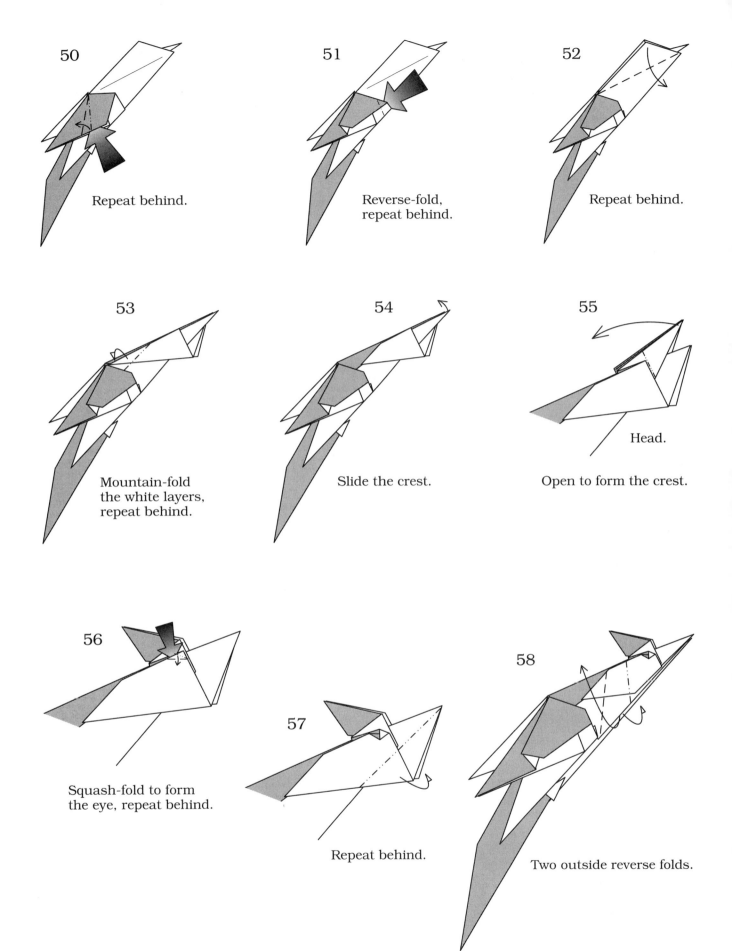

50

Repeat behind.

51

Reverse-fold,
repeat behind.

52

Repeat behind.

53

Mountain-fold
the white layers,
repeat behind.

54

Slide the crest.

55

Head.

Open to form the crest.

56

Squash-fold to form
the eye, repeat behind.

57

Repeat behind.

58

Two outside reverse folds.

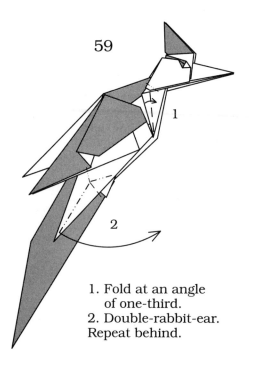

59

1. Fold at an angle
   of one-third.
2. Double-rabbit-ear.
Repeat behind.

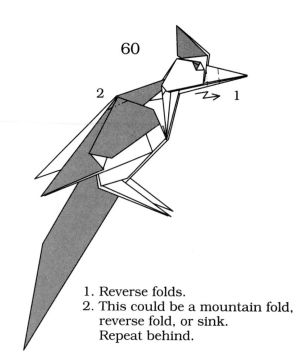

60

1. Reverse folds.
2. This could be a mountain fold,
   reverse fold, or sink.
Repeat behind.

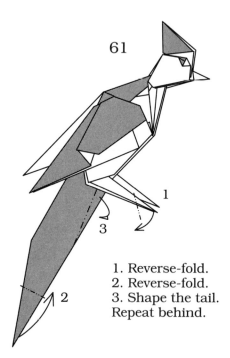

61

1. Reverse-fold.
2. Reverse-fold.
3. Shape the tail.
Repeat behind.

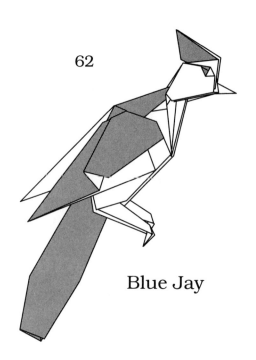

62

Blue Jay

Skunk

The skunk is a small weasellike animal that lives in the forest. It is most well known for its black and white markings and the foul smelling liquid it produces when frightened or angered. The yellowish liquid, called musk, is sprayed from the skunk's tail as far as 12 feet and smells for days. The skunk does not spray without warning. If it is bothered, it stamps its front feet, growls, or hisses before spraying. There are three main types of skunks: striped, hog-nosed, and spotted. The skunk here is the well known striped skunk, which is the most common species of skunk in the United States.

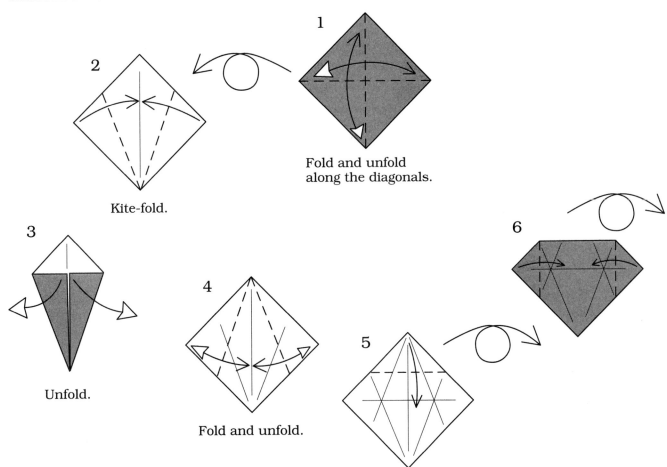

1

Fold and unfold along the diagonals.

2

Kite-fold.

3

Unfold.

4

Fold and unfold.

5

6

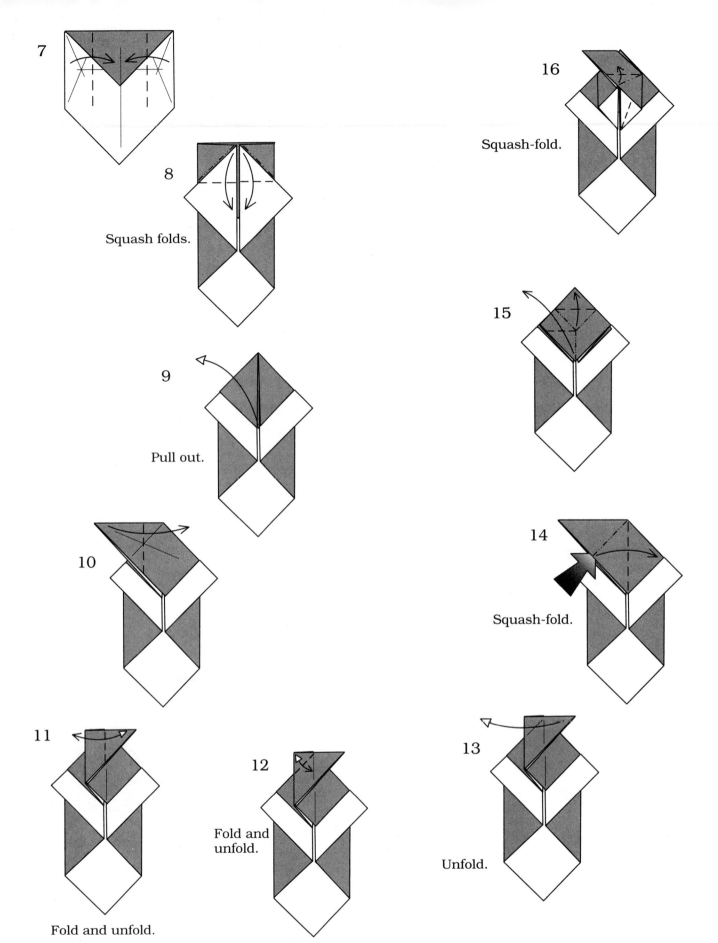

7

8

Squash folds.

9

Pull out.

10

Fold and unfold.

11

Fold and unfold.

12

Fold and unfold.

13

Unfold.

14

Squash-fold.

15

16

Squash-fold.

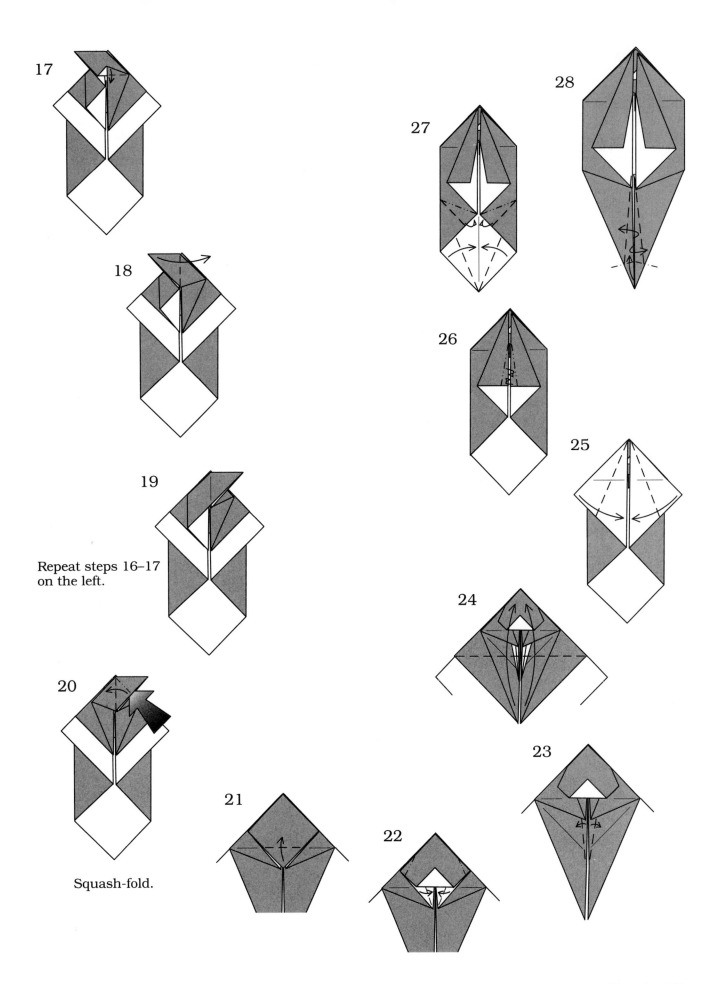

17

18

19

Repeat steps 16–17
on the left.

20

Squash-fold.

21

22

23

24

25

26

27

28

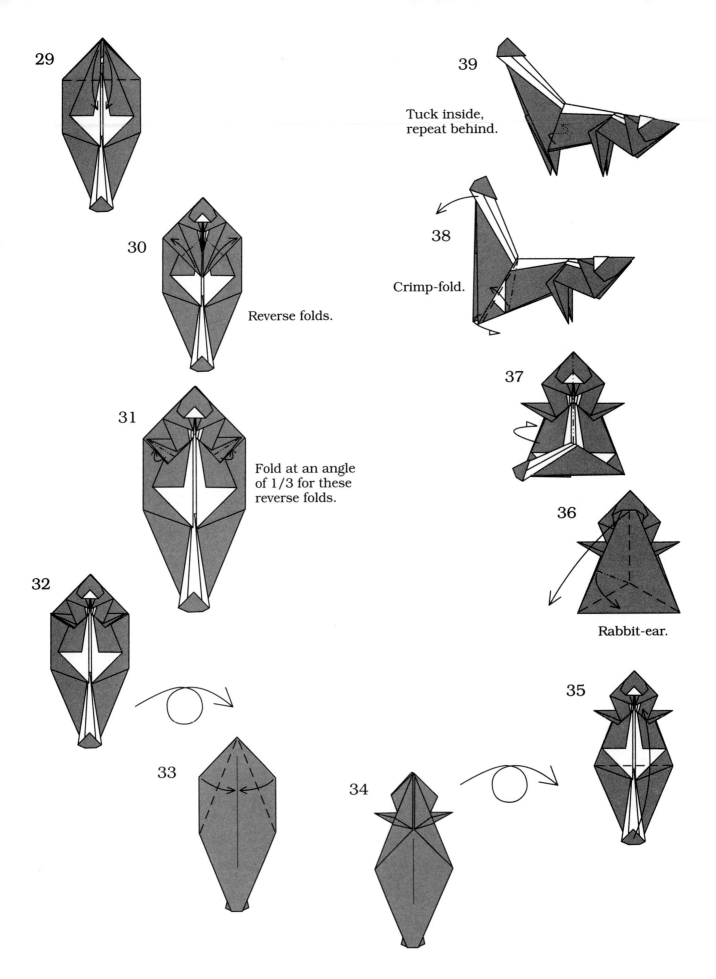

29

30

Reverse folds.

31

Fold at an angle
of 1/3 for these
reverse folds.

32

33

34

35

36

Rabbit-ear.

37

38

Crimp-fold.

39

Tuck inside,
repeat behind.

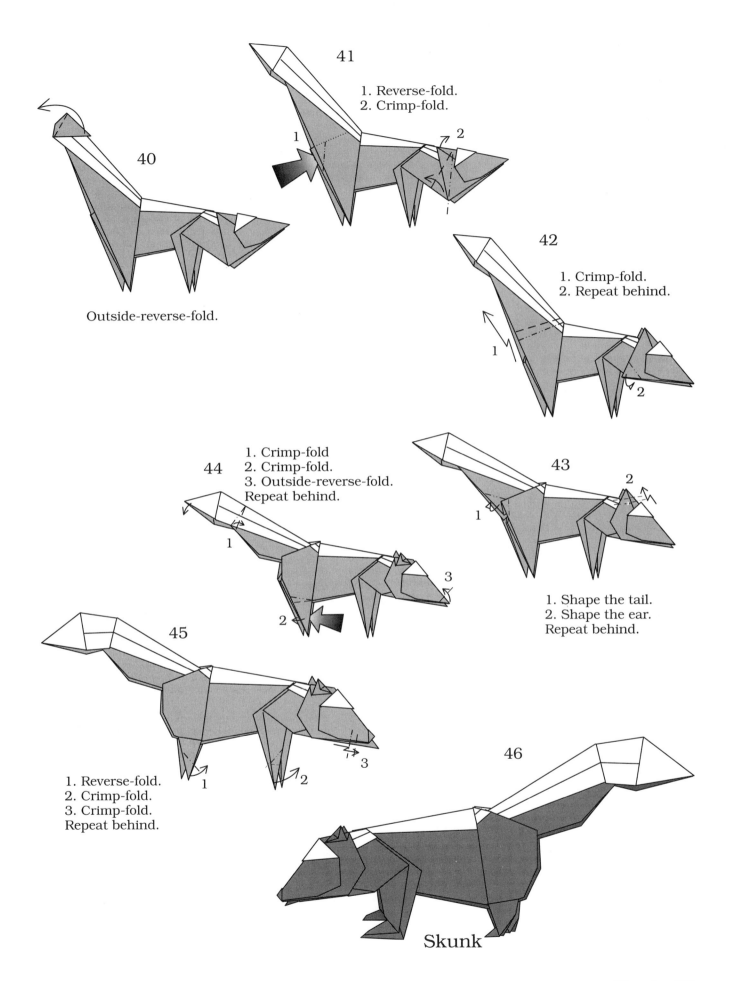

40

Outside-reverse-fold.

41

1. Reverse-fold.
2. Crimp-fold.

42

1. Crimp-fold.
2. Repeat behind.

43

1. Shape the tail.
2. Shape the ear.
Repeat behind.

44

1. Crimp-fold
2. Crimp-fold.
3. Outside-reverse-fold.
Repeat behind.

45

1. Reverse-fold.
2. Crimp-fold.
3. Crimp-fold.
Repeat behind.

46

Skunk

Anteater

Ode to the Anteater

Whatever one says, it's impossible to kiss
An anteater so short and squat;
For there's this terribly long proboscis
That this eater of ants has got.
He sticks his honker down in a hole,
And then with a deadly "slurp",
All of the ants are sucked from their home
And become nothing but . . . BUUURRRRP!

Tim Getman

1

Fold and unfold.

2

3

Fold and unfold,
repeat behind.

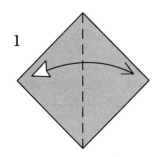

4

Fold up and unfold
creasing lightly.

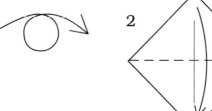

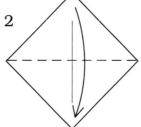

5

Fold up and unfold
creasing lightly.

6

Fold up and unfold
creasing lightly.

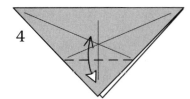

7

Fold up almost to the line.

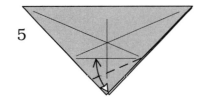

8

Fold and unfold.

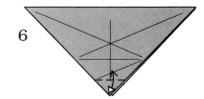

9

Fold and unfold.

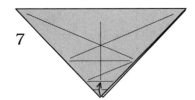

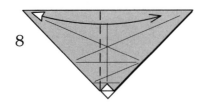

10

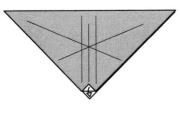

Unfold.

11

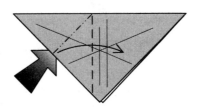

Squash-fold.

12

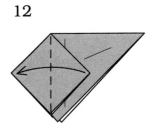

13

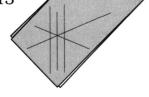

Repeat steps 11–12 on the right.

14

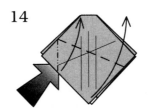

Squash-fold.

15

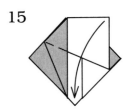

16

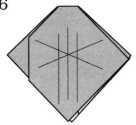

Repeat steps 14–15 on the right and behind.

17

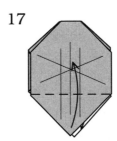

Repeat behind.

18

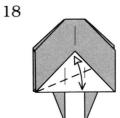

Fold down and unfold, crease lightly.

19

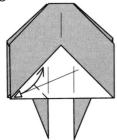

Fold up and unfold, crease lightly.

20

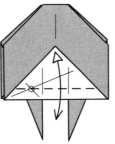

Fold down and unfold, crease lightly.

21

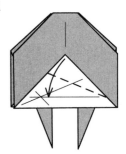

Fold down to the line.

22

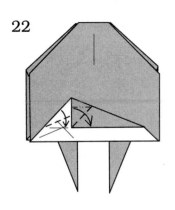

Squash-fold.

23

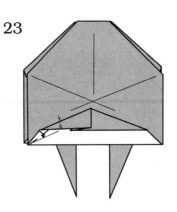

Fold to the crease line.

24

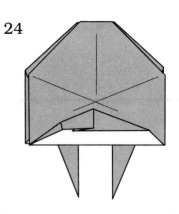

Repeat steps 18–23 behind in its mirror image.

25

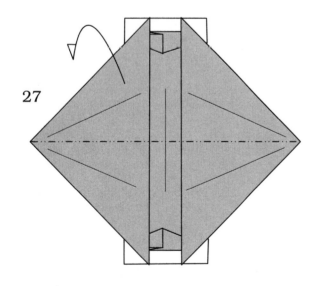

Unfold.

26

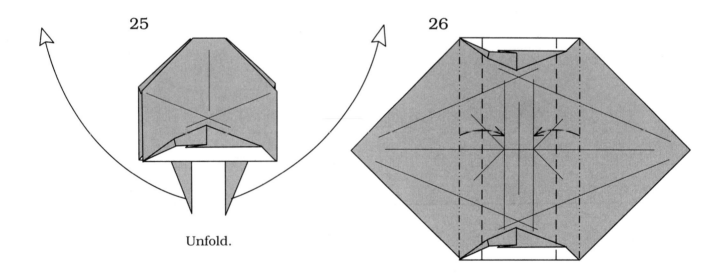

27

28

29

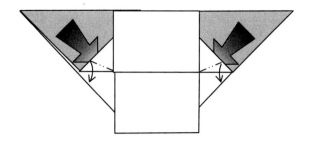

30

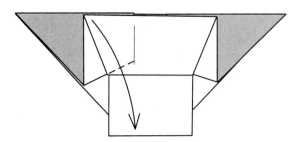

Only crease on the left side.

31

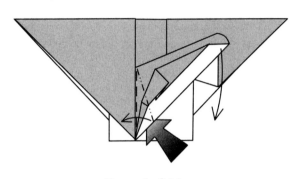

Squash-fold.

32

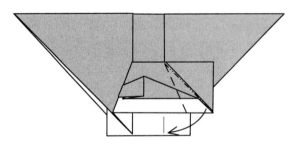

33

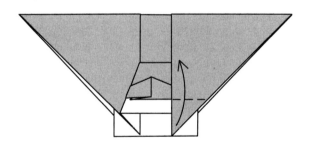

Crease lightly.

34

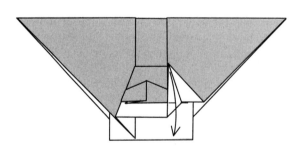

35

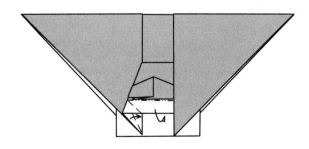

36

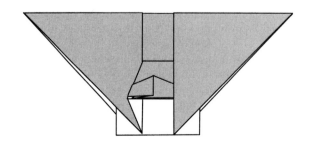

Repeat steps 28–35 behind.

Anteater 61

37

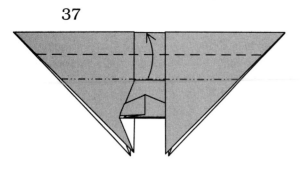

Repeat behind.

38

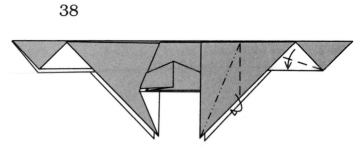

Repeat behind.

39

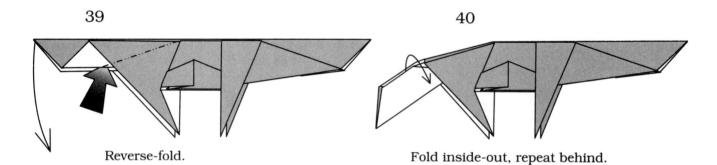

Reverse-fold.

40

Fold inside-out, repeat behind.

41

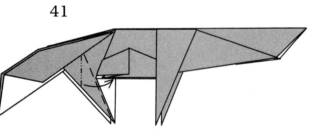

Repeat behind.

42

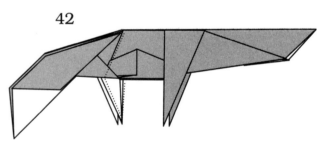

Place the lower layer
on top. Repeat behind.

43

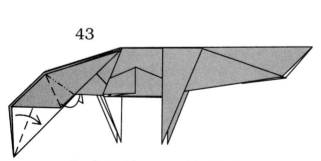

Tuck inside, repeat behind.

44

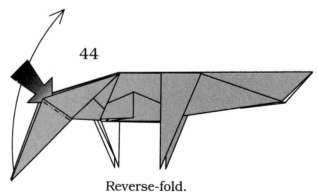

Reverse-fold.

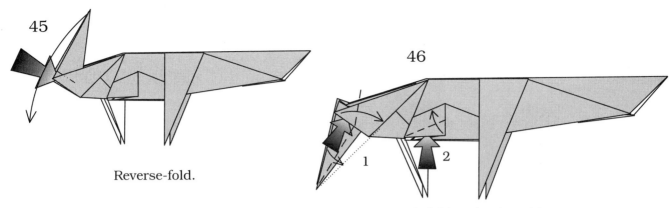

45

Reverse-fold.

46

1. Squash-fold to the dotted line.
2. Squash-fold.
Repeat behind.

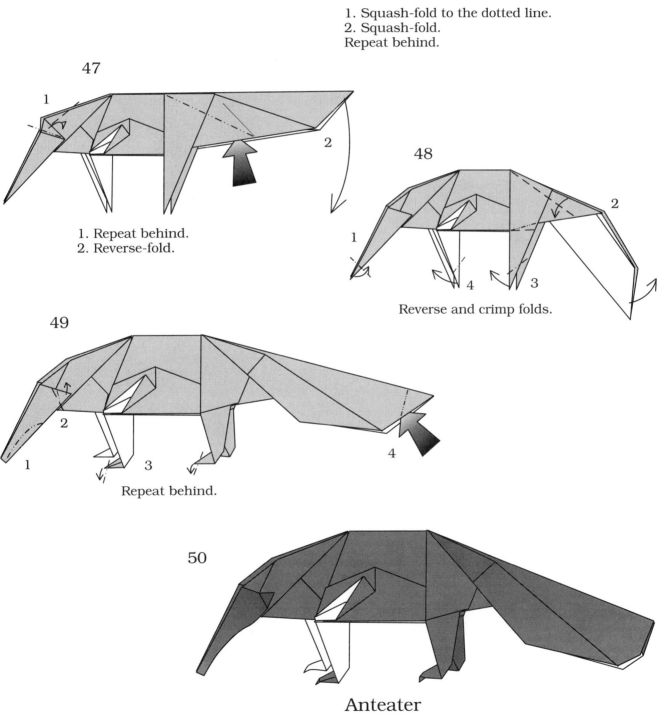

47

1. Repeat behind.
2. Reverse-fold.

48

Reverse and crimp folds.

49

Repeat behind.

50

Anteater

Raccoon

A raccoon is a furry animal with a bushy tail and a band of black hair around its eyes which resembles a mask. An adult raccoon measures around three feet in length and can weigh from twelve to twenty-five pounds.

Raccoons enjoy eating crabs, frogs, fish, bird's eggs, acorns, fruits, and a variety of other foods. A raccoon finds this food on its home range. A home range is the name given to the habitat, or living area, which a raccoon occupies. Usually these home ranges are about 200 acres, and the raccoon is able to do whatever is necessary to survive in this area.

Raccoons are also known for their mischief. Raccoons can be a serious nuisance and are able to scratch through almost anything with their feet. Oddly enough, each one of their feet resembles a human hand, and raccoons are even able to manipulate their food with ease. Ironically, though, raccoons can be enjoyed as pets. They are said to be smarter than cats and easily trained, but unfortunately, by the age of one, they become very short tempered and begin to scratch and bite.

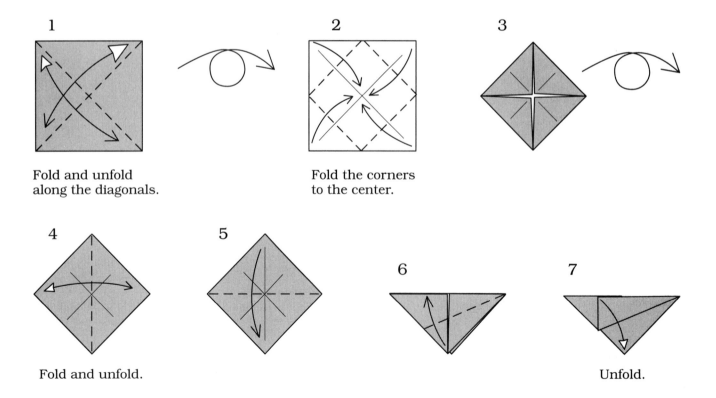

1
Fold and unfold along the diagonals.

2
Fold the corners to the center.

3

4
Fold and unfold.

5

6

7
Unfold.

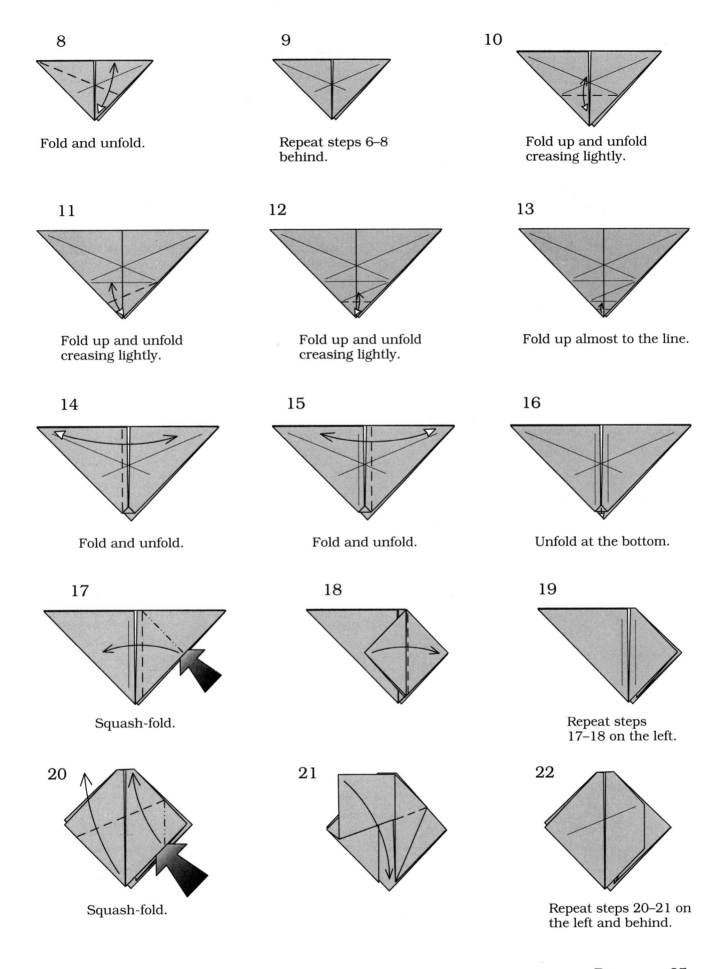

8

Fold and unfold.

9

Repeat steps 6–8 behind.

10

Fold up and unfold creasing lightly.

11

Fold up and unfold creasing lightly.

12

Fold up and unfold creasing lightly.

13

Fold up almost to the line.

14

Fold and unfold.

15

Fold and unfold.

16

Unfold at the bottom.

17

Squash-fold.

18

19

Repeat steps 17–18 on the left.

20

Squash-fold.

21

22

Repeat steps 20–21 on the left and behind.

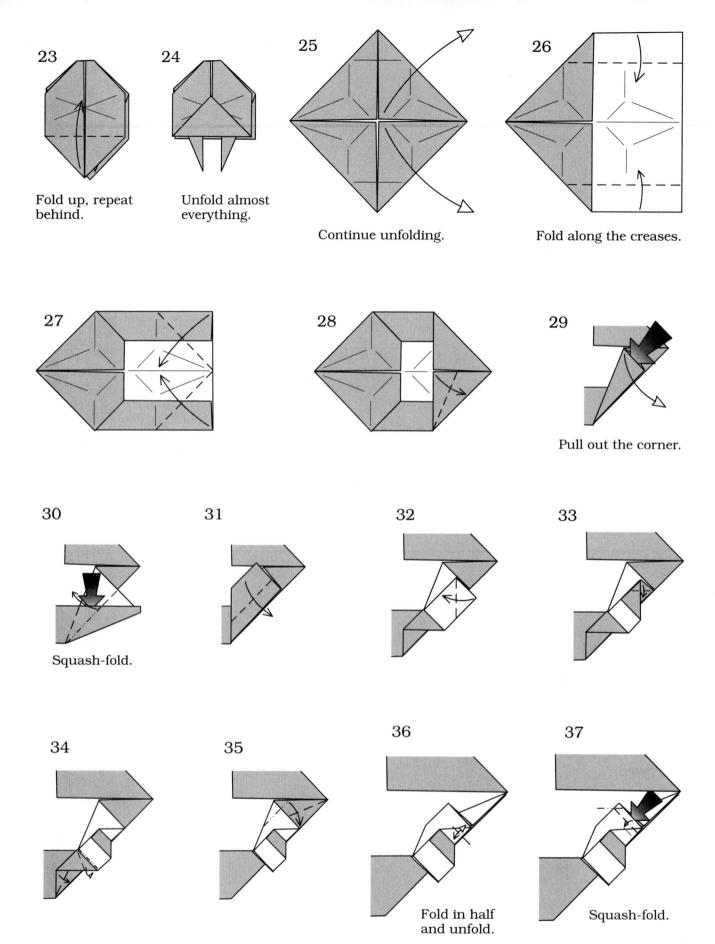

23 Fold up, repeat behind.

24 Unfold almost everything.

25 Continue unfolding.

26 Fold along the creases.

27

28

29 Pull out the corner.

30 Squash-fold.

31

32

33

34

35

36 Fold in half and unfold.

37 Squash-fold.

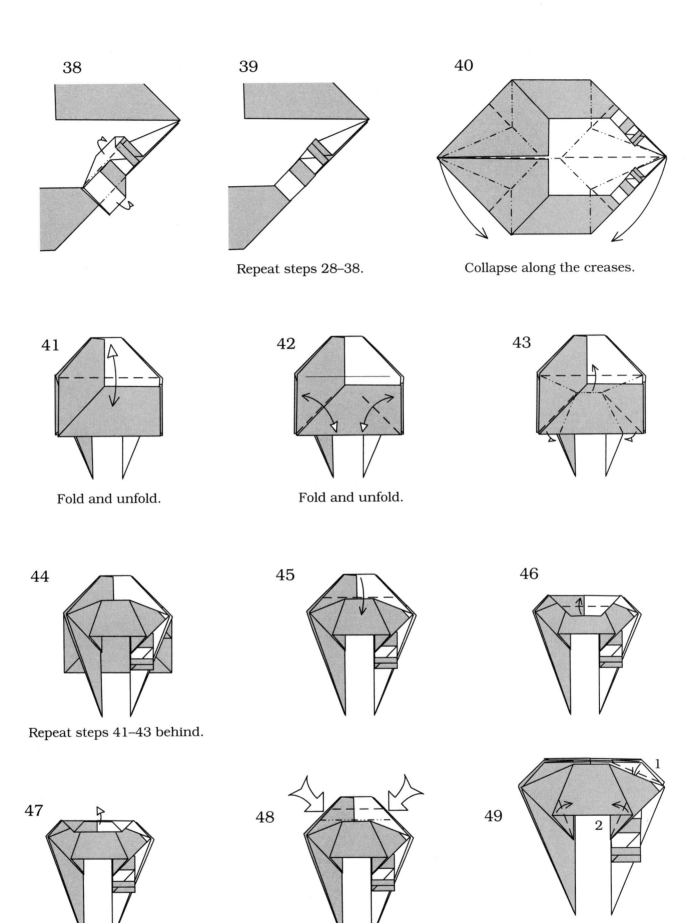

38

39

Repeat steps 28–38.

40

Collapse along the creases.

41

Fold and unfold.

42

Fold and unfold.

43

44

Repeat steps 41–43 behind.

45

46

47

Unfold.

48

Sink down and up.

49

Tuck inside at 1.
Repeat behind.

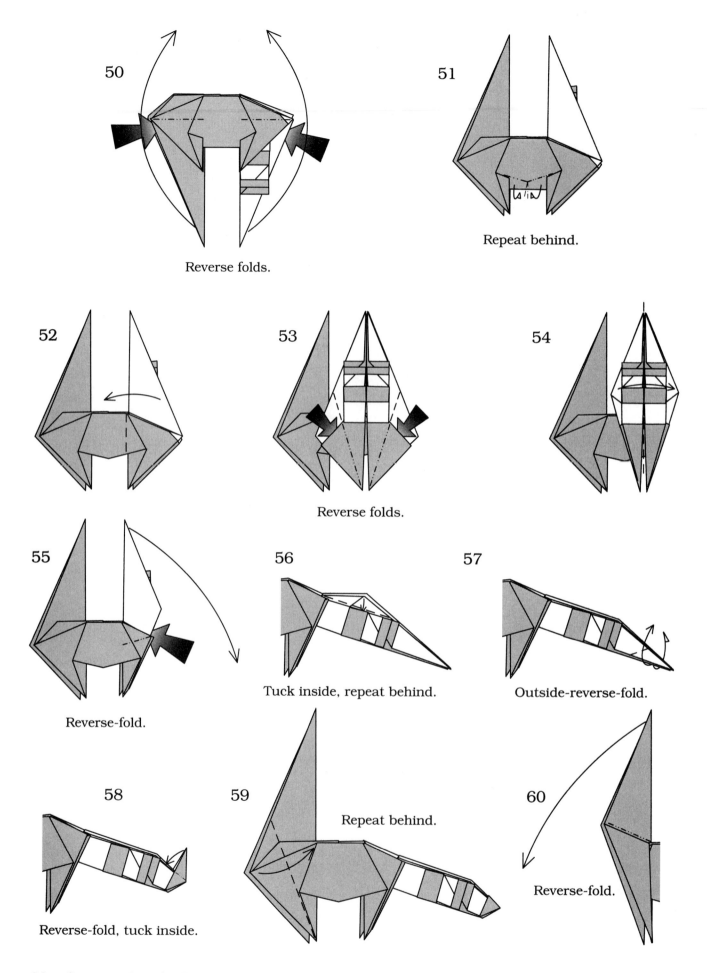

50

Reverse folds.

51

Repeat behind.

52

53

Reverse folds.

54

55

Reverse-fold.

56

Tuck inside, repeat behind.

57

Outside-reverse-fold.

58

Reverse-fold, tuck inside.

59

Repeat behind.

60

Reverse-fold.

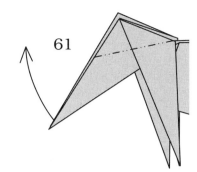

61

Reverse-fold.

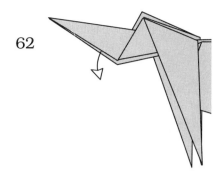

62

Pull out, repeat behind.

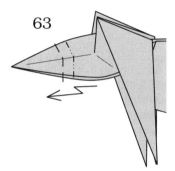

63

The head is three-dimensional.
Reverse folds.

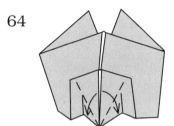

64

Front view.

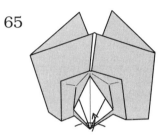

65

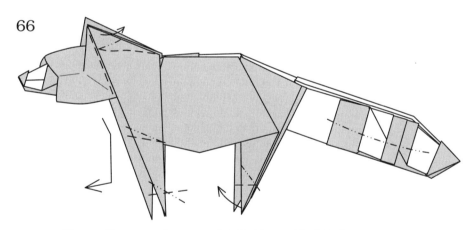

66

Shape the ears, legs, and tail. Repeat behind.

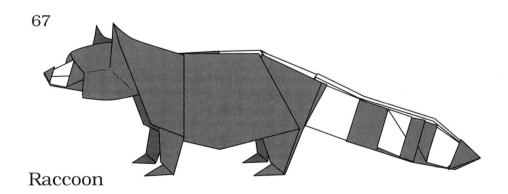

67

Raccoon

Tiger

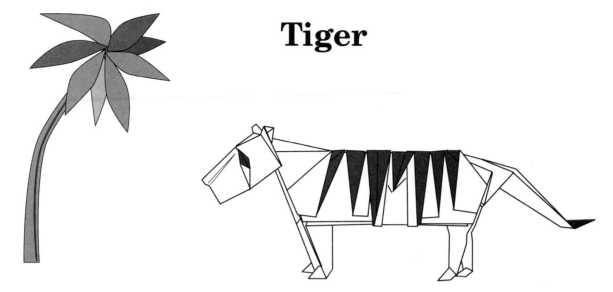

The tiger is the largest member of the cat family. Its strength, beauty, and ferocity are unrivalled among cats. Tigers may grow to be in excess of 10 feet long and 3 feet tall. Full grown males may weigh over 600 pounds. The largest sub-species is the Siberian tiger, found in the snowy reaches of Siberia. Tigers' coats, striped with distinctive black slashes on orange and white, are among the most stunning coats of the cat family.

Tigers are solitary hunters. They usually hunt at night, using excellent hearing and vision. Their prey consists mainly of larger animals—deer, antelope, wild oxen, and boar. Although most cats dislike water, tigers often take to water on hot days. Tigers have ranges extending over 250 square miles.

Once found throughout Asia, tigers are now only in selected areas of India, Russia, China, and Indonesia. Tiger numbers have greatly dwindled since 1900, when 40,000 were found in India alone. Today, only 4,000 remain in India. Tigers can be seen in most zoos.

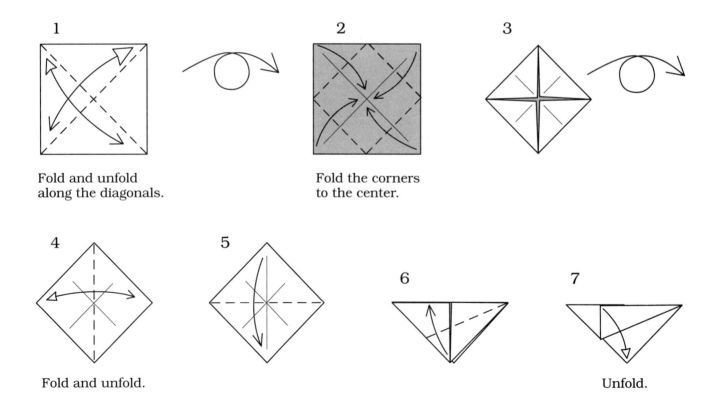

1

Fold and unfold
along the diagonals.

2

Fold the corners
to the center.

3

4

Fold and unfold.

5

6

7

Unfold.

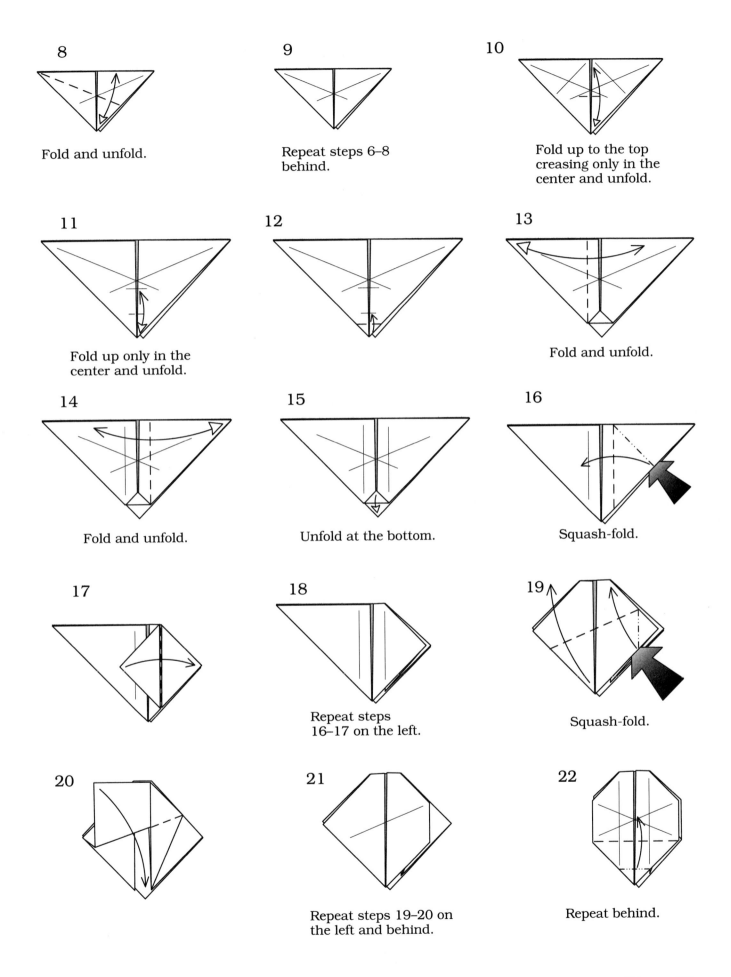

8

Fold and unfold.

9

Repeat steps 6–8 behind.

10

Fold up to the top creasing only in the center and unfold.

11

Fold up only in the center and unfold.

12

13

Fold and unfold.

14

Fold and unfold.

15

Unfold at the bottom.

16

Squash-fold.

17

18

Repeat steps 16–17 on the left.

19

Squash-fold.

20

21

Repeat steps 19–20 on the left and behind.

22

Repeat behind.

23

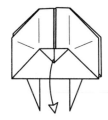

Unfold, repeat behind.

24

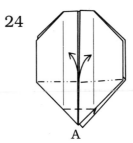

A

Fold inside with
reverse folds,
repeat behind.

25

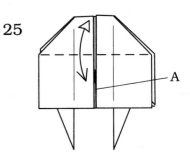

A

Fold and unfold.

26

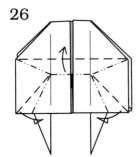

27

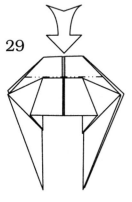

Repeat steps 25–26 behind.

28

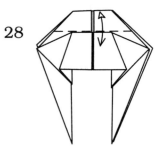

Fold and unfold.

29

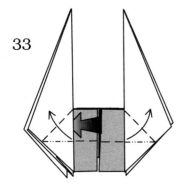

Sink.

30

Pull out the
four corners.

31

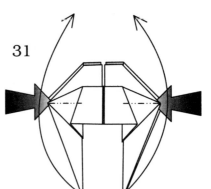

Reverse folds.

32

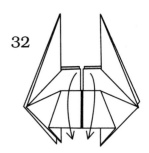

Unlock, repeat behind.

33

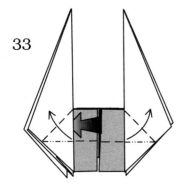

Squash folds, repeat behind.

34

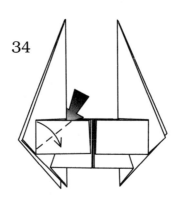

Squash-fold to form a
stripe. Repeat behind.

35

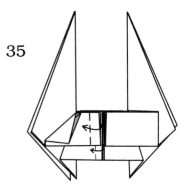

Fold four layers to make
two stripes. Repeat behind.

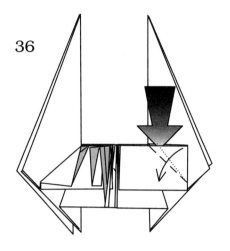

36

Squash-fold, repeat behind.

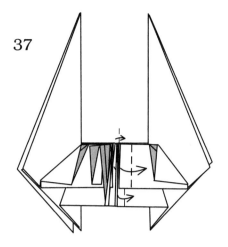

37

Fold five layers to form three stripes. Repeat behind.

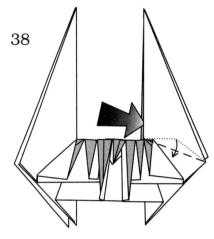

38

Tuck inside, repeat behind.

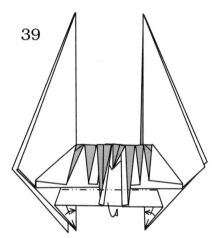

39

Repeat behind.

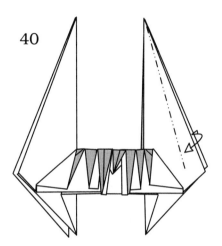

40

Fold behind at an angle of one-third. Unfold and repeat behind.

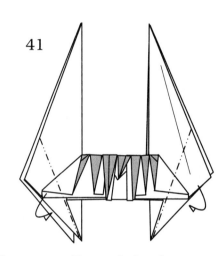

41

Repeat behind.

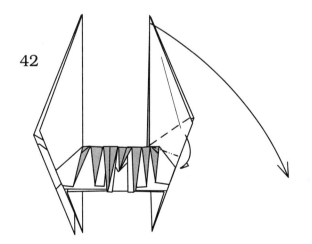

42

Crimp-fold.

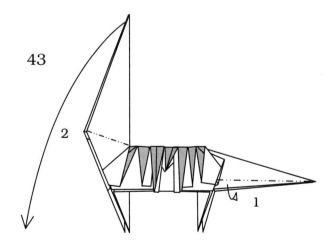

43

1. Repeat behind.
2. Reverse-fold.

44

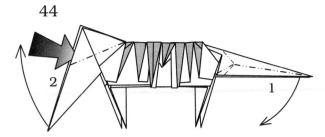

1. Double-rabbit-ear.
2. Reverse-fold.

45

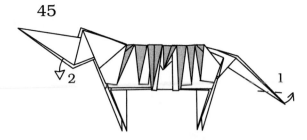

1. Reverse-fold.
2. Pull out paper,
   repeat behind.

46

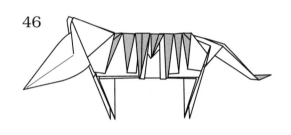

Front view of head.

47

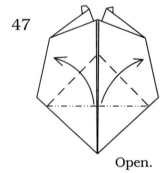

Open.

48

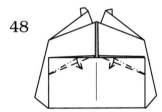

Squash folds.

49

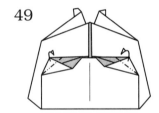

50

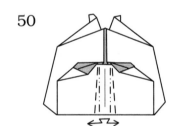

51

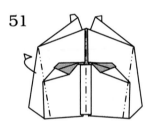

Fold the head in half. It
will be three-dimensional.

52

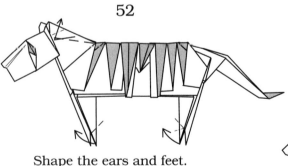

Shape the ears and feet.
Repeat behind.

53

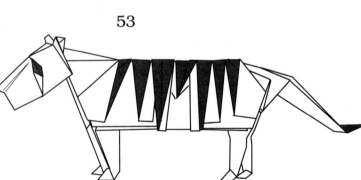

Tiger

Elephant

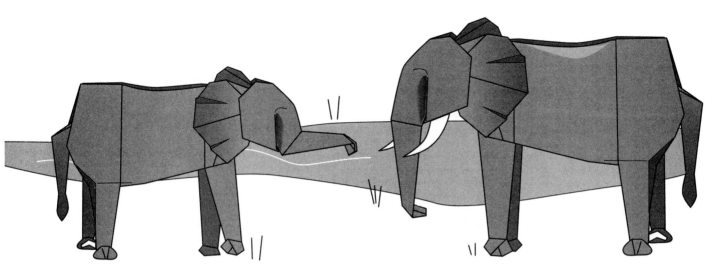

Zō-San, Zō-San
Ohana ga nagai no ne?
Sō yo, Kāsan mo
Nagai no yo.

Elephant, elephant,
Why is your nose so long?
True, my mother's nose is also
Really long!

—Japanese Children's Song

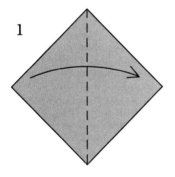

1

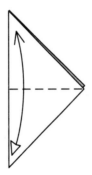

2

Fold up and unfold.

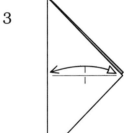

3

Fold one layer and
unfold, creasing only
at the center. Rotate.

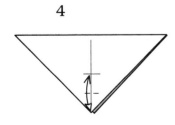

4

Fold up and unfold,
creasing only at the center.

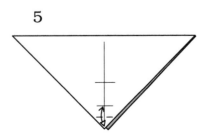

5

Fold up and unfold,
creasing only at the center.

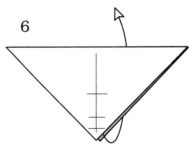

6

Unfold.

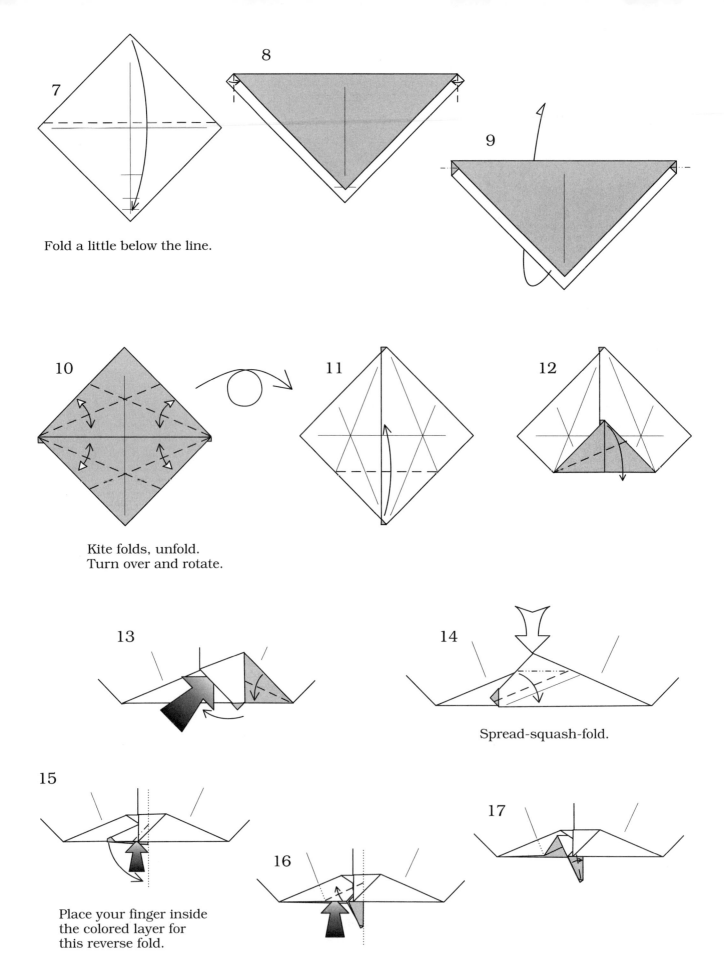

7

8

9

Fold a little below the line.

10

Kite folds, unfold.
Turn over and rotate.

11

12

13

14

Spread-squash-fold.

15

Place your finger inside
the colored layer for
this reverse fold.

16

17

18

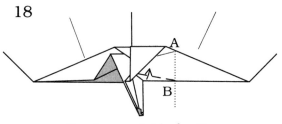

Use A as a guide for B.

19

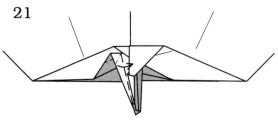

20

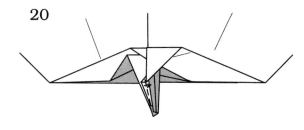

21

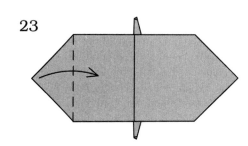

Squash-fold.

22

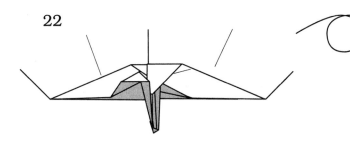

Repeat steps 10–21 to
form the other front leg.

23

24

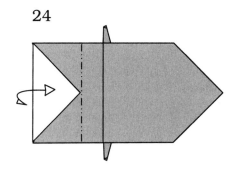

Fold behind and
unfold, crease lightly.

25

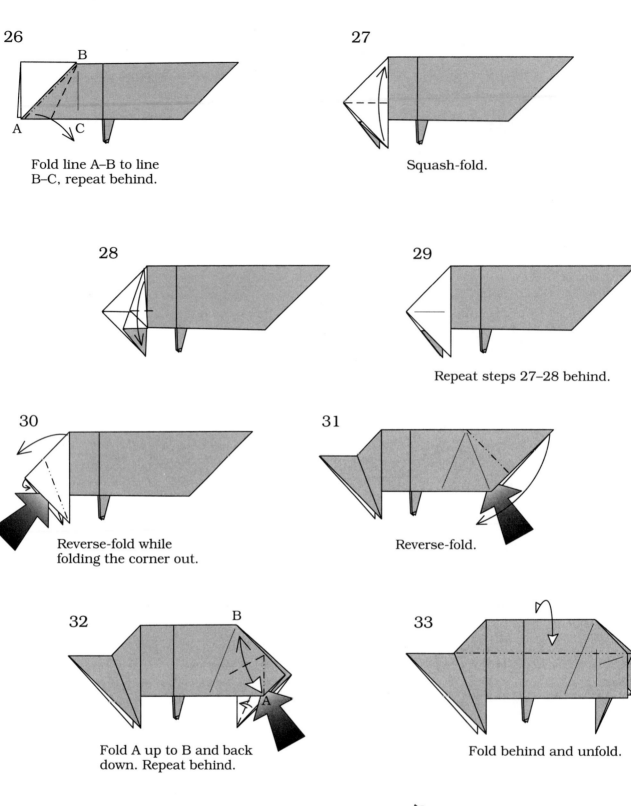

26

B

A C

Fold line A–B to line
B–C, repeat behind.

27

Squash-fold.

28

29

Repeat steps 27–28 behind.

30

Reverse-fold while
folding the corner out.

31

Reverse-fold.

32

B

A

Fold A up to B and back
down. Repeat behind.

33

Fold behind and unfold.

34

35

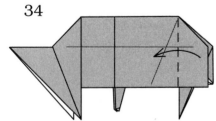

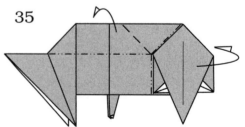

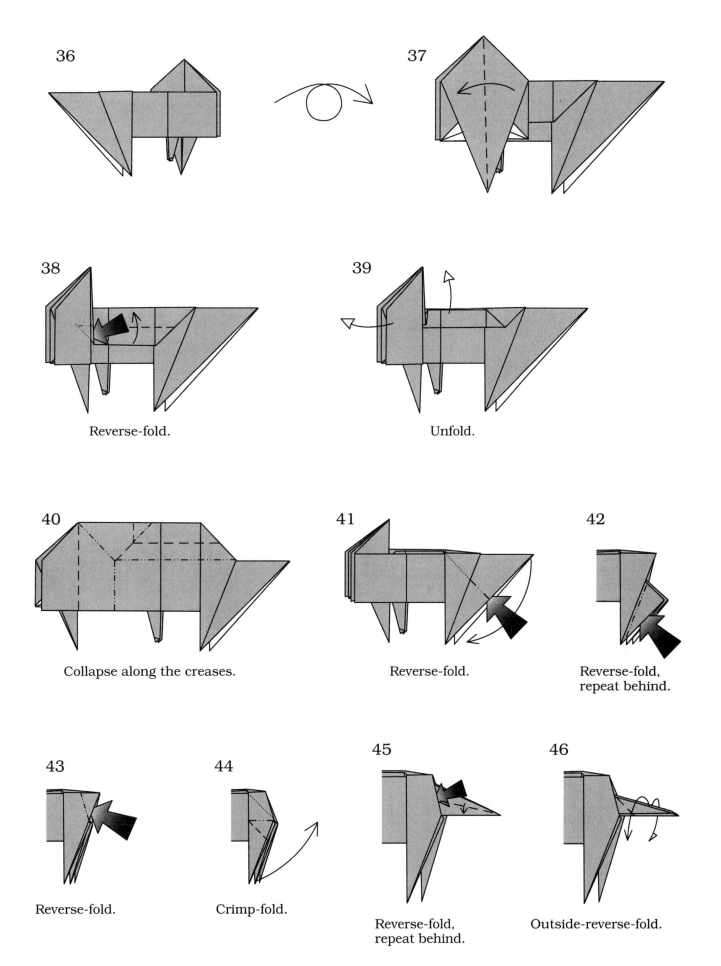

36

37

38

Reverse-fold.

39

Unfold.

40

Collapse along the creases.

41

Reverse-fold.

42

Reverse-fold,
repeat behind.

43

Reverse-fold.

44

Crimp-fold.

45

Reverse-fold,
repeat behind.

46

Outside-reverse-fold.

Elephant 79

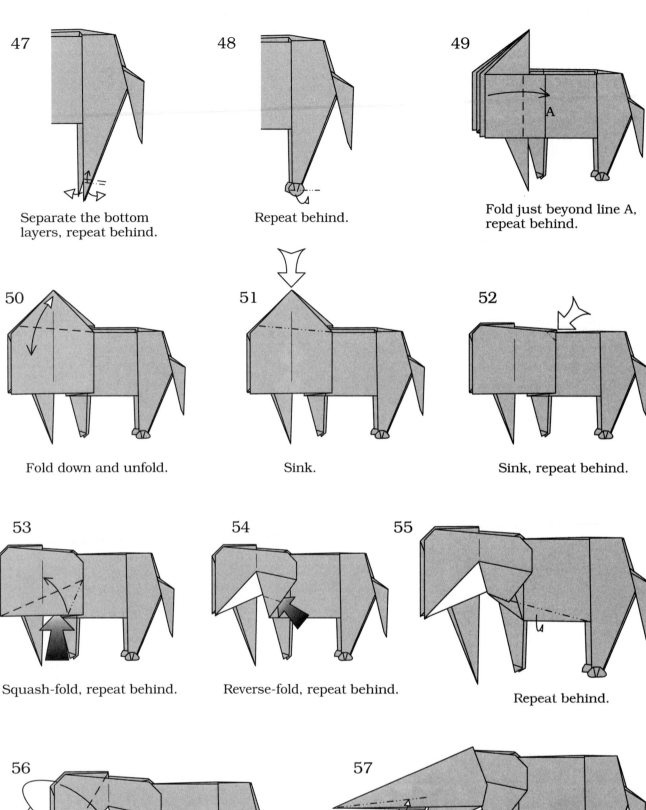

47

Separate the bottom
layers, repeat behind.

48

Repeat behind.

49

Fold just beyond line A,
repeat behind.

50

Fold down and unfold.

51

Sink.

52

Sink, repeat behind.

53

Squash-fold, repeat behind.

54

Reverse-fold, repeat behind.

55

Repeat behind.

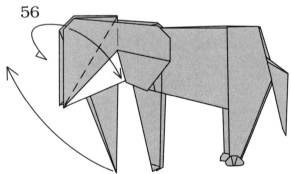

56

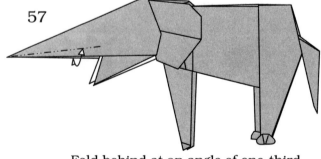

57

Fold behind at an angle of one-third,
unfold and repeat behind.

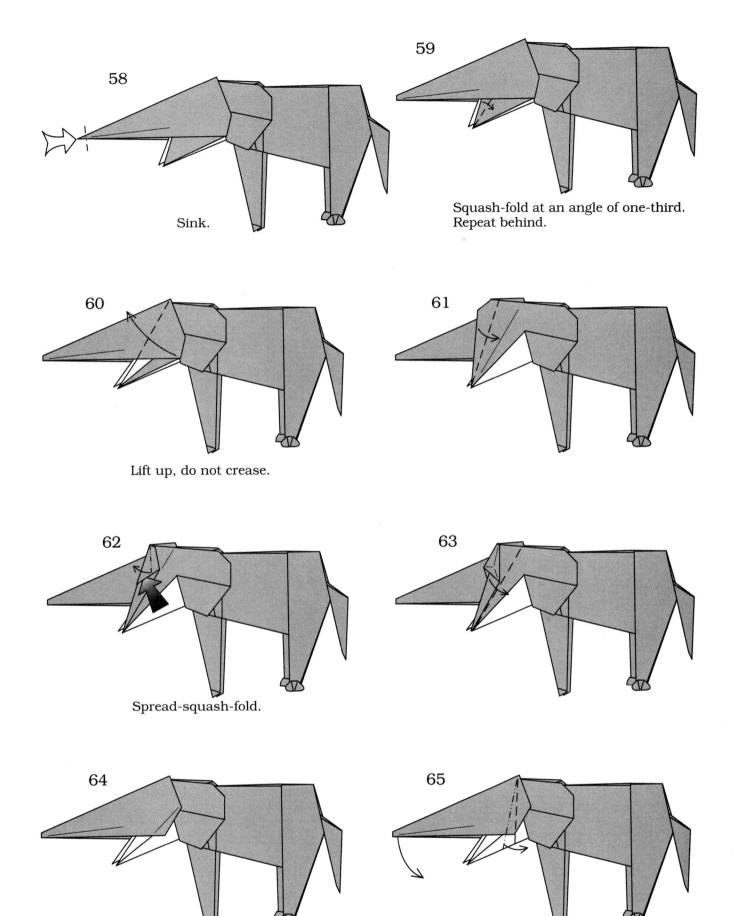

58

Sink.

59

Squash-fold at an angle of one-third.
Repeat behind.

60

Lift up, do not crease.

61

62

Spread-squash-fold.

63

64

Repeat steps 60–63 behind.

65

Crimp-fold.

66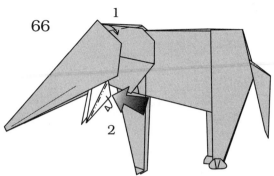

Shape the tusk and ear.
Repeat behind.

67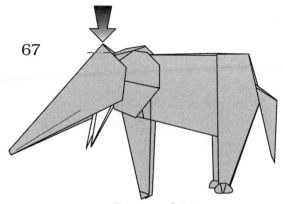

Reverse-fold.

68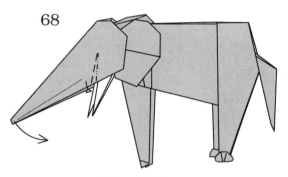

Crimp-fold.

69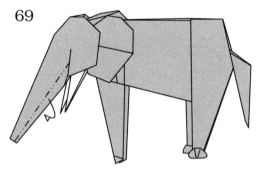

Fold at an angle of one-third along
the existing line. Repeat behind.

70

Crimp-fold the trunk. Shape
the toes, repeat behind.

71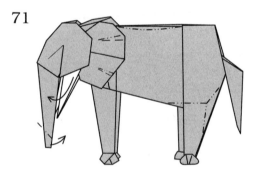

Curl the tusks up. Shape the trunk.
ears, legs, and back. Repeat behind.

72

Elephant

Holstein Cow

Ode to a Holstein Cow

I think bovines are very fine:
They dot the hills in northern climes.
Most often of the genus Bos,
Extremely gentle, rarely cross,
They consume large quantities of grass,
And pollute the air with methane gas.
There are many species that we can list:
From Jerseys and Guernseys to Brown Swiss.
Yet Holsteins are a breed apart—
Black and white, origami art.

Jeremiah Helm

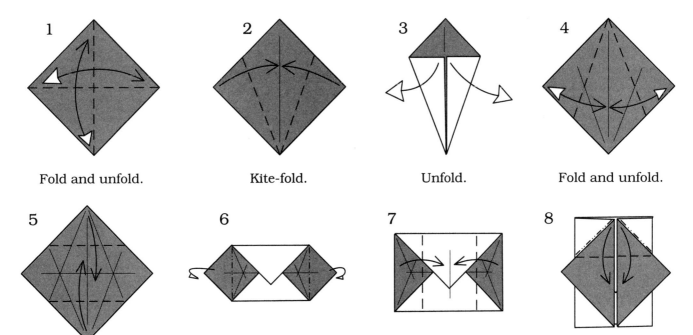

1

Fold and unfold.

2

Kite-fold.

3

Unfold.

4

Fold and unfold.

5

6

7

8

Squash folds.

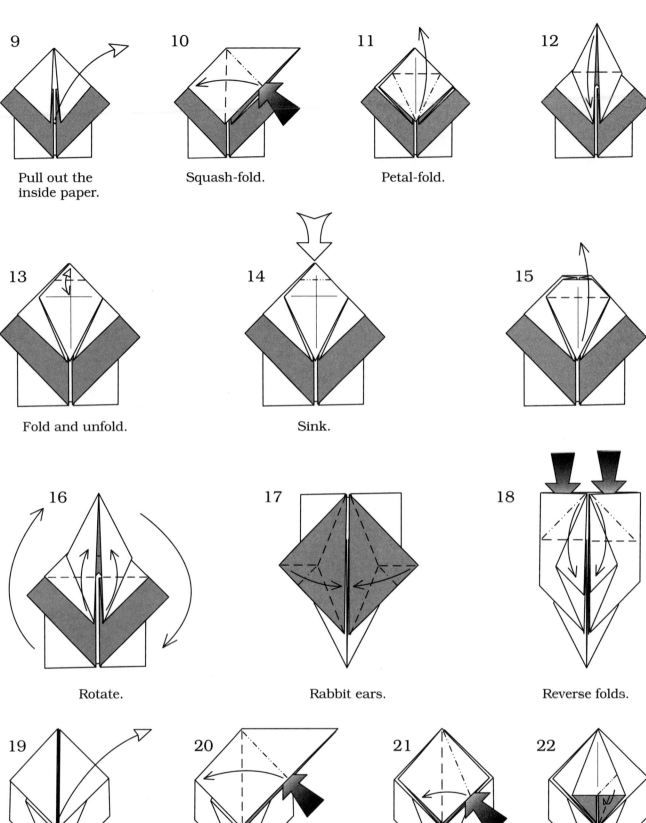

9
Pull out the
inside paper.

10
Squash-fold.

11
Petal-fold.

12

13
Fold and unfold.

14
Sink.

15

16
Rotate.

17
Rabbit ears.

18
Reverse folds.

19
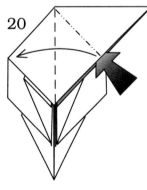
Pull out the inside paper.

20
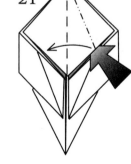
Squash-fold.

21
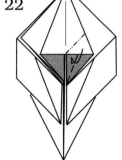
Squash-fold.

22

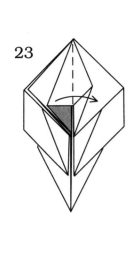

23

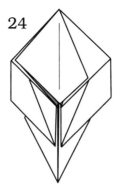

24

Repeat steps
21–23 on the left.

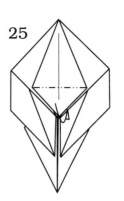

25

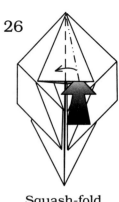

26

Squash-fold.

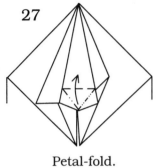

27

Petal-fold.

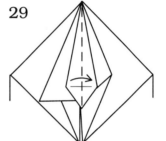

28

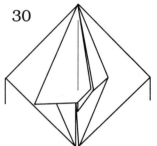

29

30

Repeat steps
26–29 on the left.

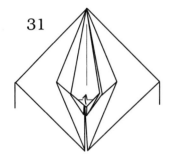

31

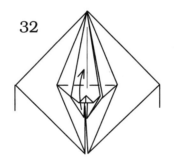

32

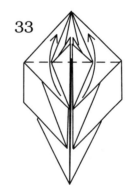

33

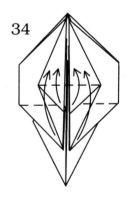

34

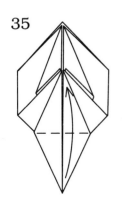

35

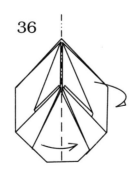

36

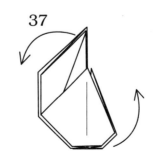

37

Rotate.

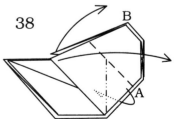

38

Fold A inside and to
the left, repeat behind
at the same time.

39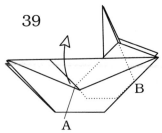

Repeat behind.

40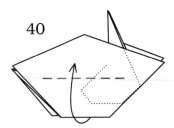

Lift up to squash-fold
the udder. Do not
crease the top layer.

41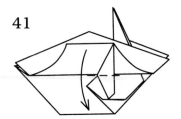

42

Repeat steps 40–41 behind.

43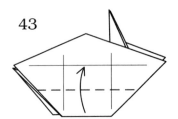

44

*The folding is no longer symmetric.
Be sure to orient your model along
with the diagrams.*

45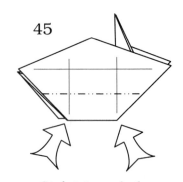

Sink triangularly.

46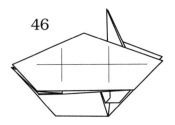

47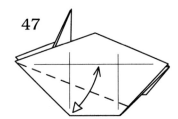

Fold and unfold.

48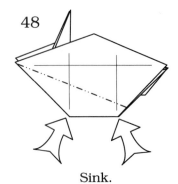

Sink.

49

Repeat behind.

50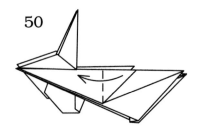

Repeat behind.

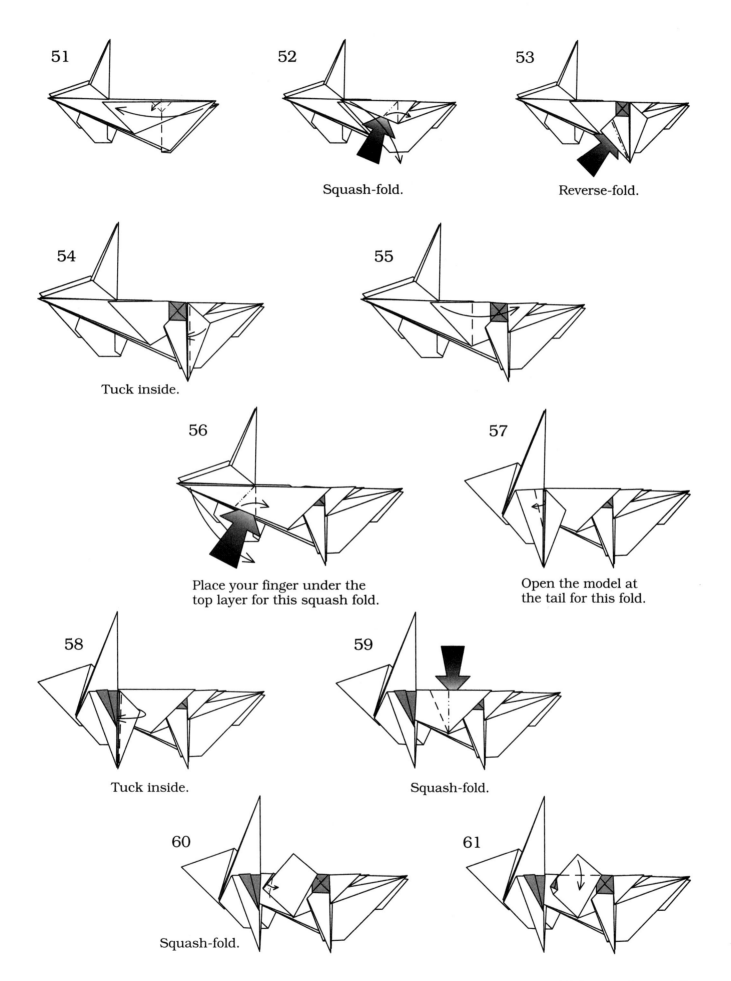

51

52

Squash-fold.

53

Reverse-fold.

54

Tuck inside.

55

56

Place your finger under the
top layer for this squash fold.

57

Open the model at
the tail for this fold.

58

Tuck inside.

59

Squash-fold.

60

Squash-fold.

61

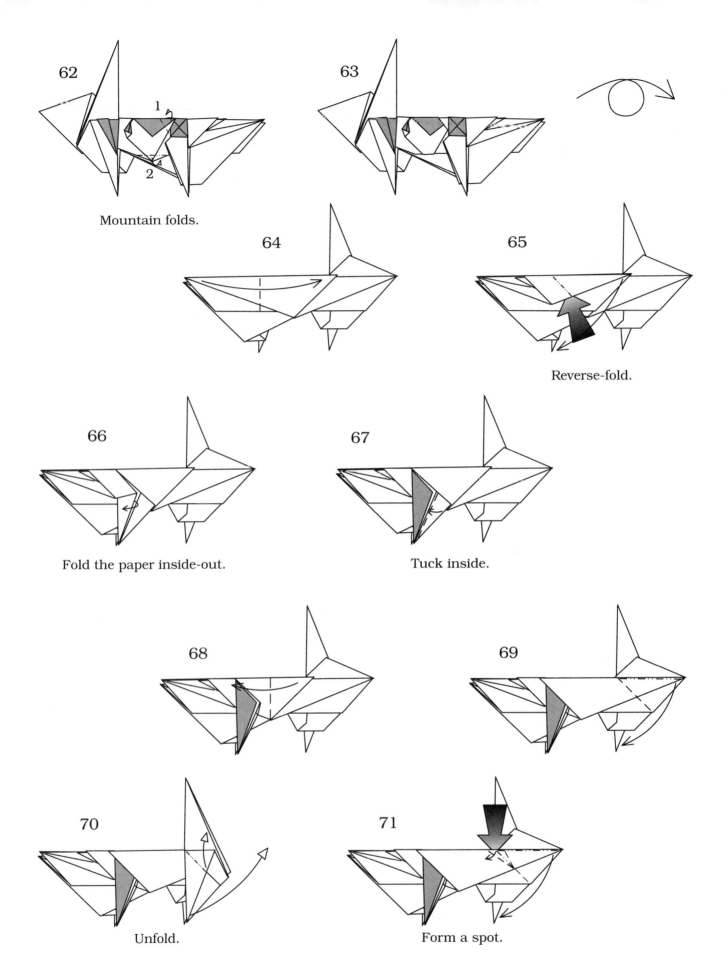

62

63

Mountain folds.

64

65

Reverse-fold.

66

67

Fold the paper inside-out.

Tuck inside.

68

69

70

71

Unfold.

Form a spot.

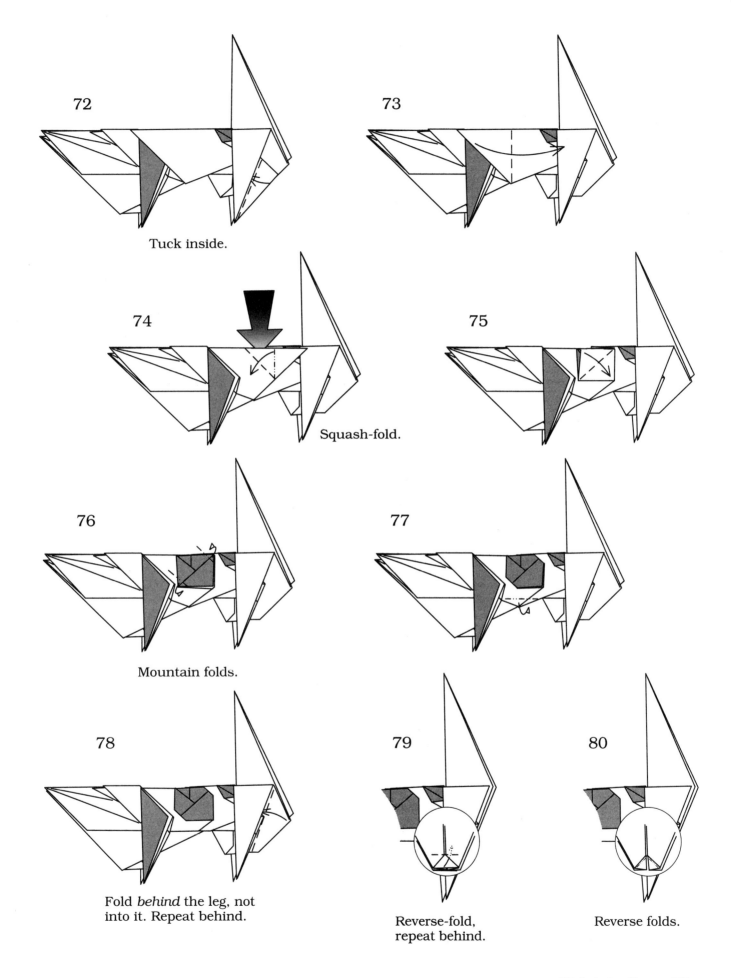

72

Tuck inside.

73

74

Squash-fold.

75

76

Mountain folds.

77

78

Fold *behind* the leg, not
into it. Repeat behind.

79

Reverse-fold,
repeat behind.

80

Reverse folds.

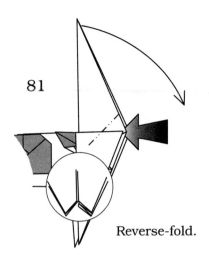

81

Reverse-fold.

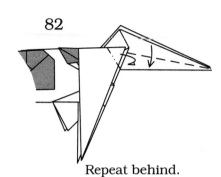

82

Repeat behind.

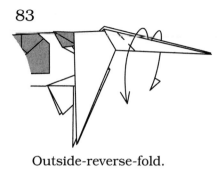

83

Outside-reverse-fold.

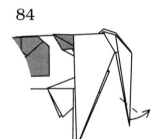

84

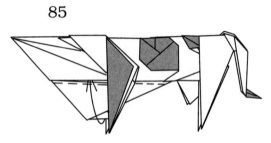

85

Tuck inside to lock the body.

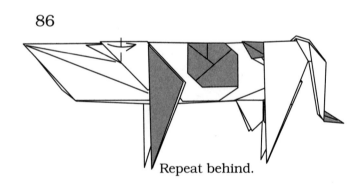

86

Repeat behind.

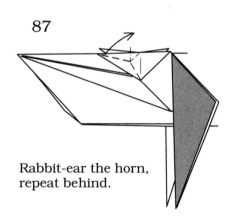

87

Rabbit-ear the horn,
repeat behind.

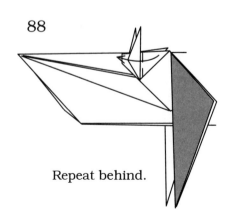

88

Repeat behind.

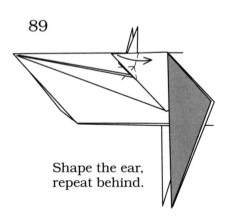

89

Shape the ear,
repeat behind.

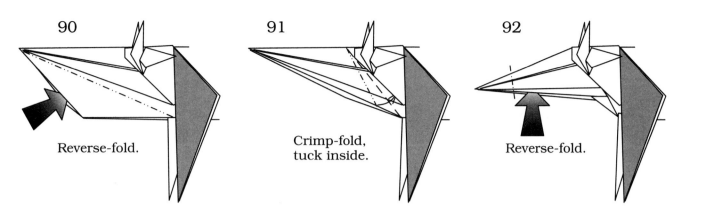

90

Reverse-fold.

91

Crimp-fold,
tuck inside.

92

Reverse-fold.

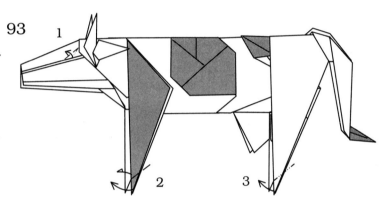

93

1. Shape the eyes, if possible.
2. Outside-reverse-fold only
   one leg.
3. Inside-reverse-fold the
   remaining three legs.

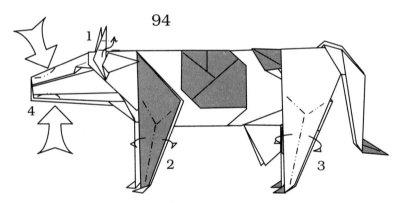

94

1. Shape the horns.
2 & 3. Thin the legs.
4. Shape the head.
Repeat behind.

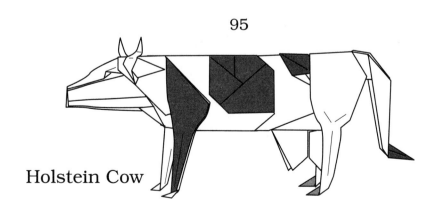

95

Holstein Cow

Chess—Game of Kings

Chess originated in South Asia, where a game known as "chaturanga" was played. Starting in the 5th Century A.D., chess was played in its present form in Persia. It was known as "shahmat," a word meaning "the king is dead". This is still its name in several modern languages and is the ancestor of the English word "checkmate".

According to legend, a Persian and an Arab king were fighting a bloody war, until both sides were exhausted. The kings agreed to a pact. Each would be required to invent a game, and if the other could not learn how to play, he would be required to forfeit half his kingdom. The Arabian king sent the ancient equivalent of checkers, which was easily understood by the Persian king, due to the uniformity of the pieces.

A response from the Persian king was necessary, so he invented and sent the game of chess. The complexity of the different pieces was such that the Arab king could not grasp the game. The Persian king agreed not to take half his kingdom, if the Arab agreed to a proposition. Starting with one grain of rice, it had to be doubled for every square on the chess board. Mathematically, this is one less than 2 to the 63rd power. The Arab king quickly agreed to give up half his kingdom.

Today, chess is played world-wide and may be described as the foremost game on the planet. Competitions are held regularly, and players are ranked on a point system. The elite of the chess world are the Grandmasters.

Anyone can quickly learn to play, and endless hours of entertainment can be found in the intricacies of chess.

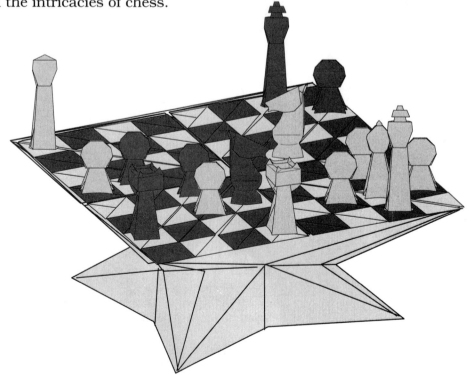

Pawn

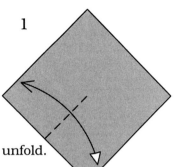

1

Fold and unfold.

2

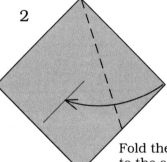

Fold the corner
to the center line.

3

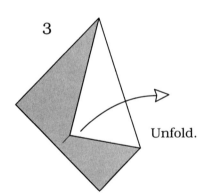

Unfold.

9

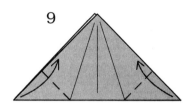

8

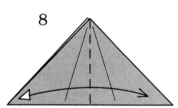

Fold in half and unfold.

7

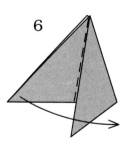

Unfold.

4

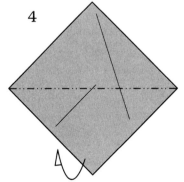

6

5

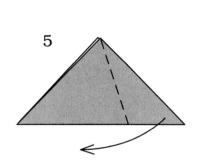

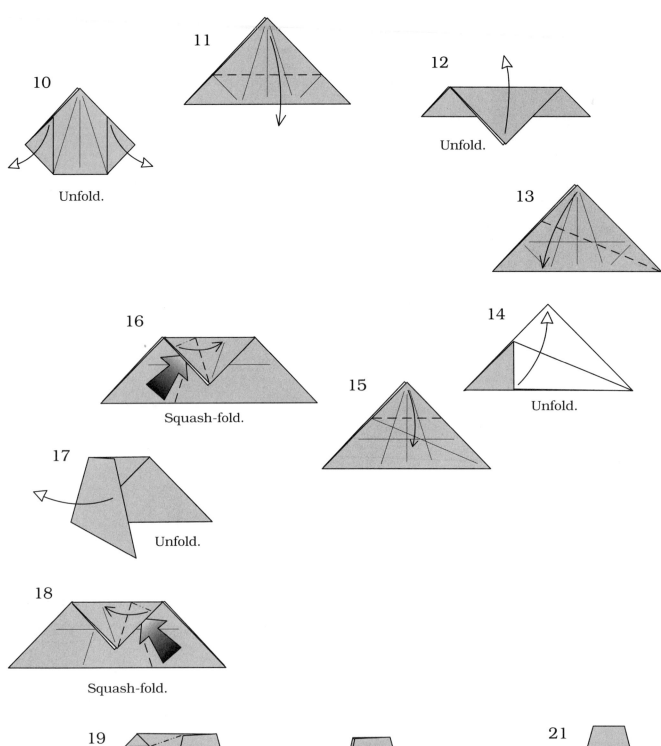

10

Unfold.

11

12

Unfold.

13

14

Unfold.

15

16

Squash-fold.

17

Unfold.

18

Squash-fold.

19

Squash-fold and tuck inside.

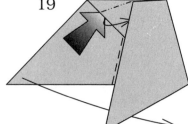

20

Fold all the layers in half
and unfold, creasing only
the bottom half.

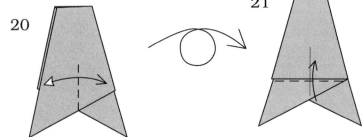

21

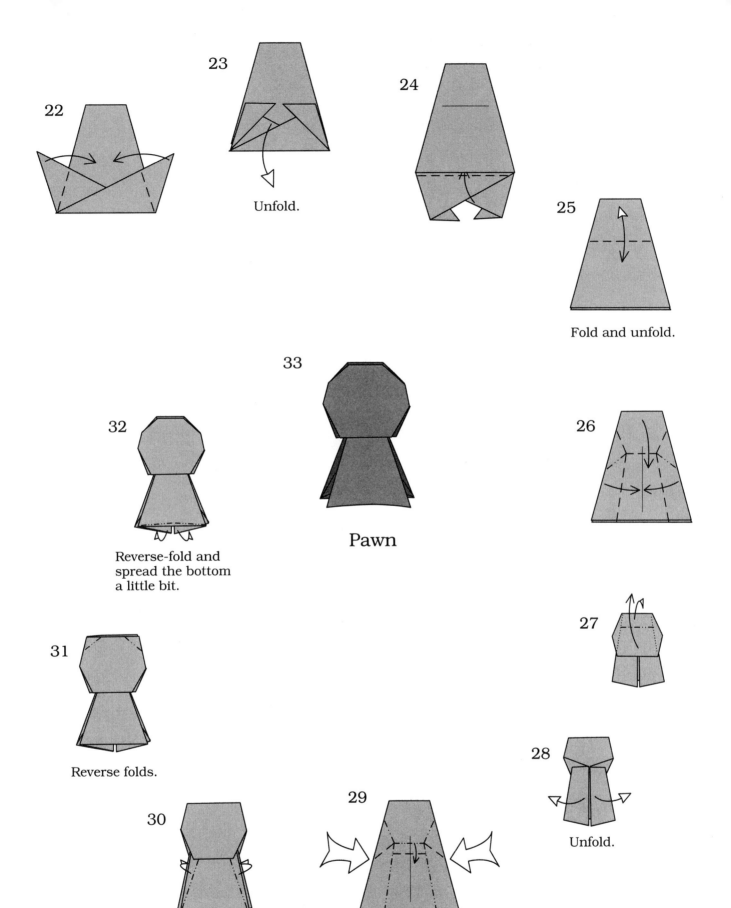

22

23

Unfold.

24

25

Fold and unfold.

33

Pawn

32

Reverse-fold and
spread the bottom
a little bit.

26

27

31

Reverse folds.

28

Unfold.

30

Repeat behind.

29

Knight

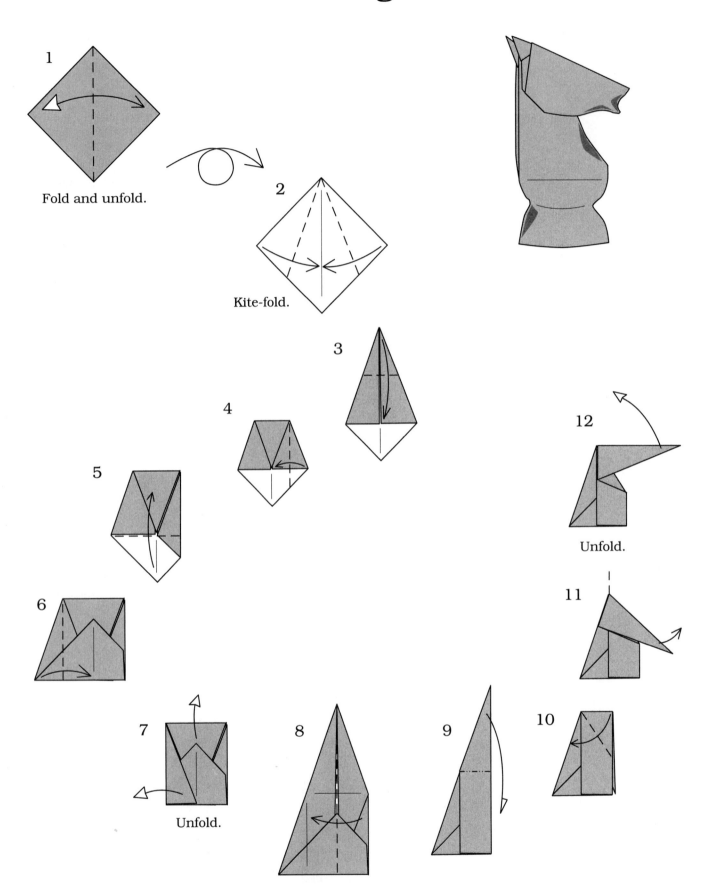

1 Fold and unfold.

2 Kite-fold.

3

4

5

6

7 Unfold.

8

9

10

11

12 Unfold.

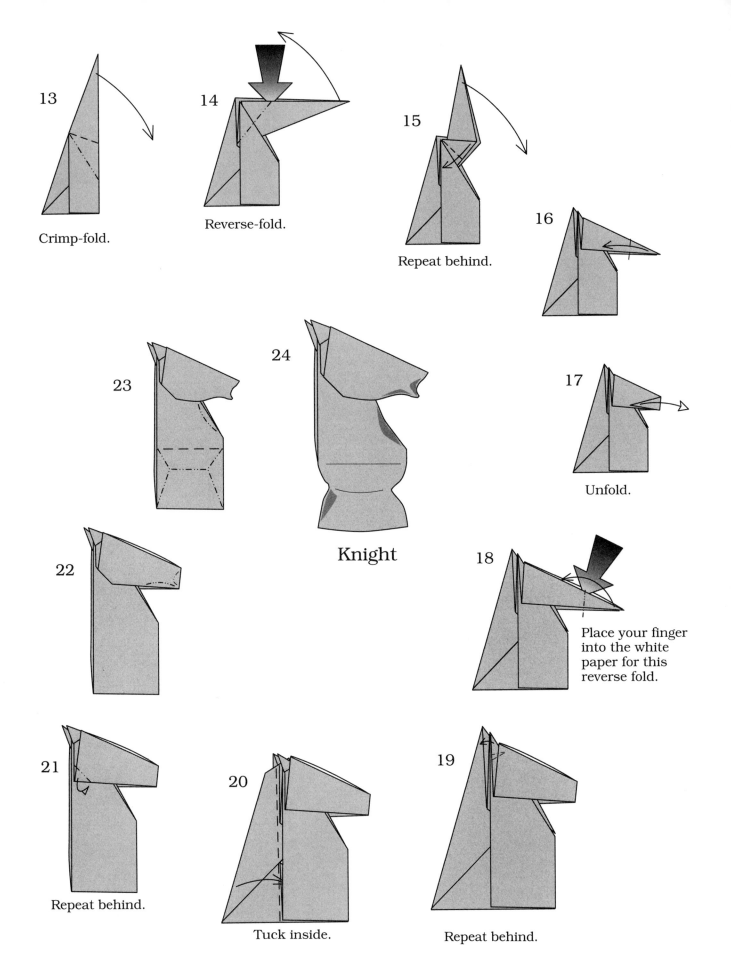

13

Crimp-fold.

14

Reverse-fold.

15

Repeat behind.

16

17

Unfold.

18

Place your finger into the white paper for this reverse fold.

19

Repeat behind.

20

Tuck inside.

21

Repeat behind.

22

23

24

Knight

Bishop

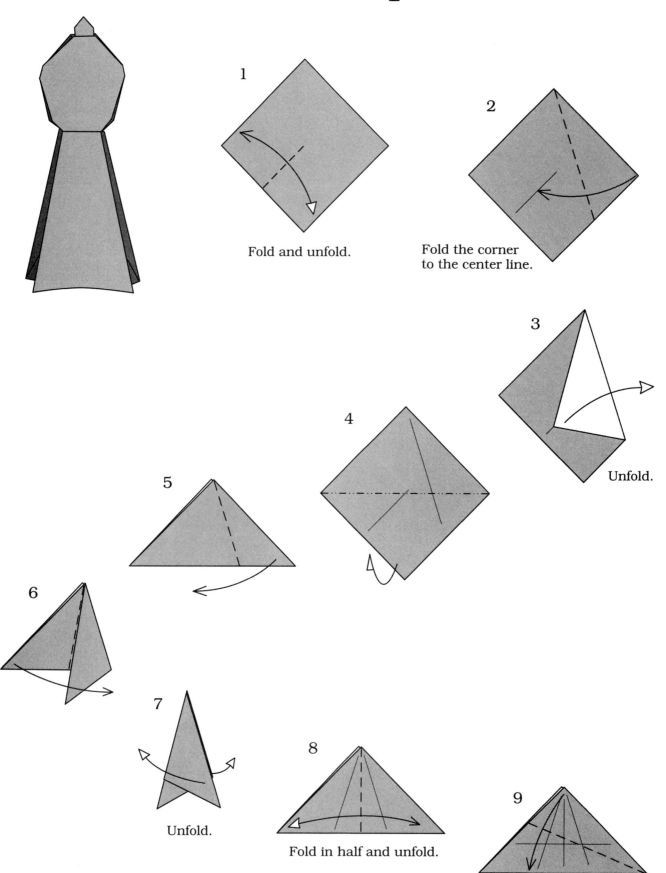

1 Fold and unfold.

2 Fold the corner to the center line.

3 Unfold.

4

5

6

7 Unfold.

8 Fold in half and unfold.

9

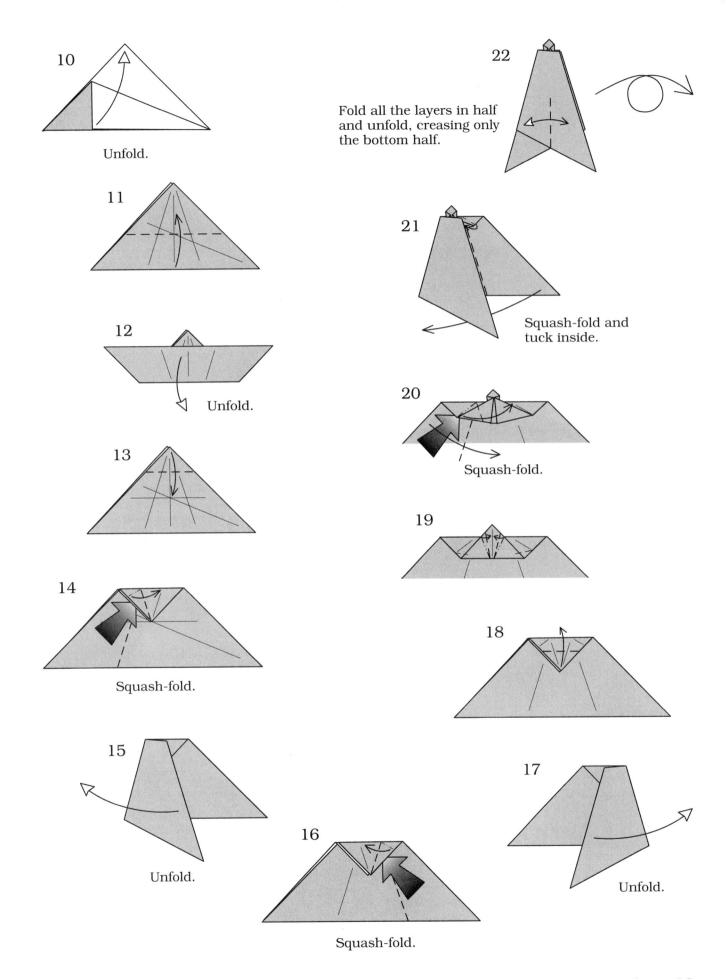

10 Unfold.

11

12 Unfold.

13

14 Squash-fold.

15 Unfold.

16 Squash-fold.

17 Unfold.

18

19

20 Squash-fold.

21 Squash-fold and tuck inside.

22 Fold all the layers in half and unfold, creasing only the bottom half.

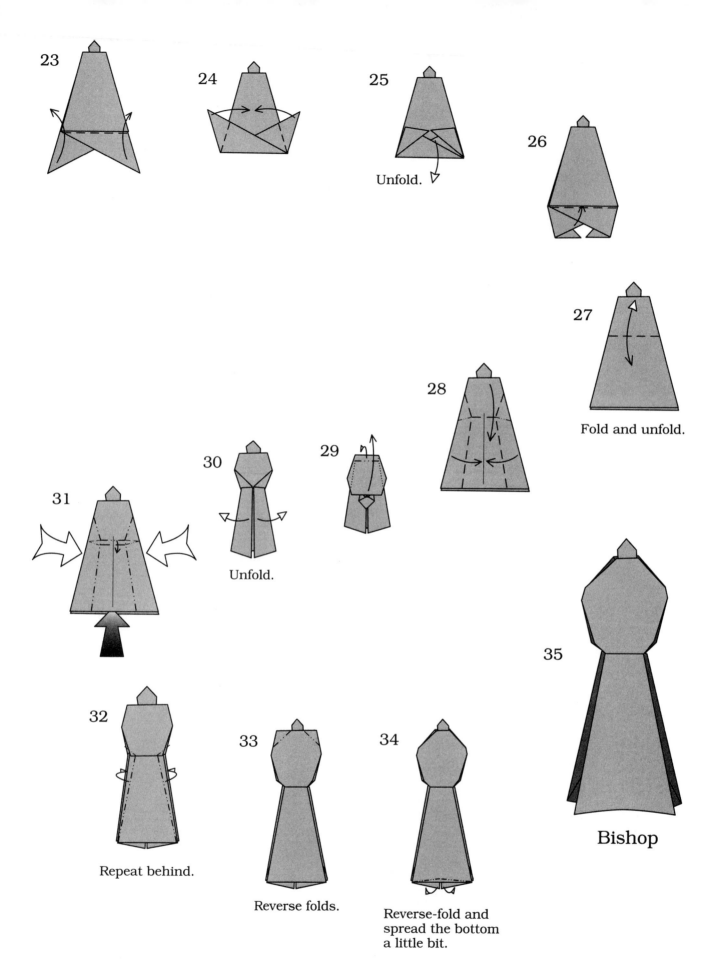

23

24

25

26

27

Fold and unfold.

28

30

Unfold.

29

31

32

Repeat behind.

33

Reverse folds.

34

Reverse-fold and
spread the bottom
a little bit.

35

Bishop

Rook

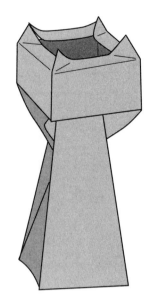

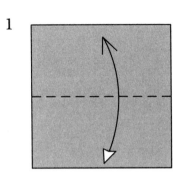

1

Fold and unfold.

2

3

4

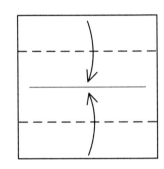

Unfold.

5

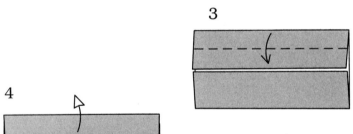

Divide in thirds.

6

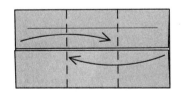

Unfold.

7

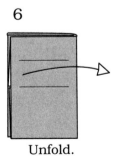

Tuck inside.

8

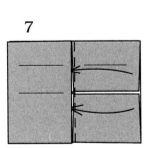

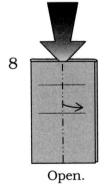

Open.

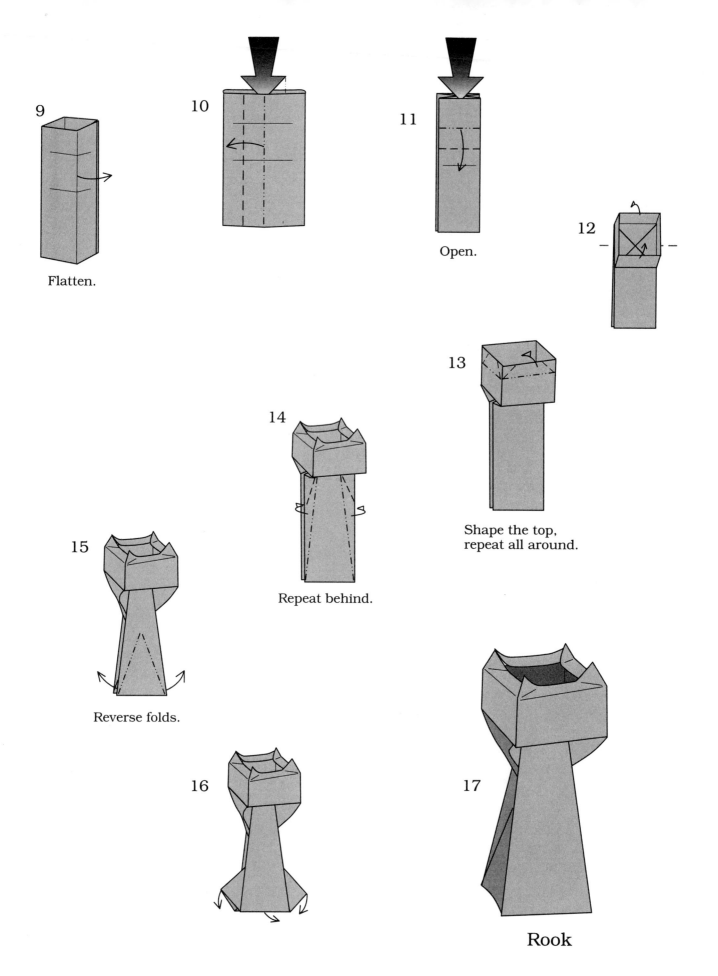

9

Flatten.

10

11

Open.

12

13

Shape the top,
repeat all around.

14

Repeat behind.

15

Reverse folds.

16

17

Rook

Queen

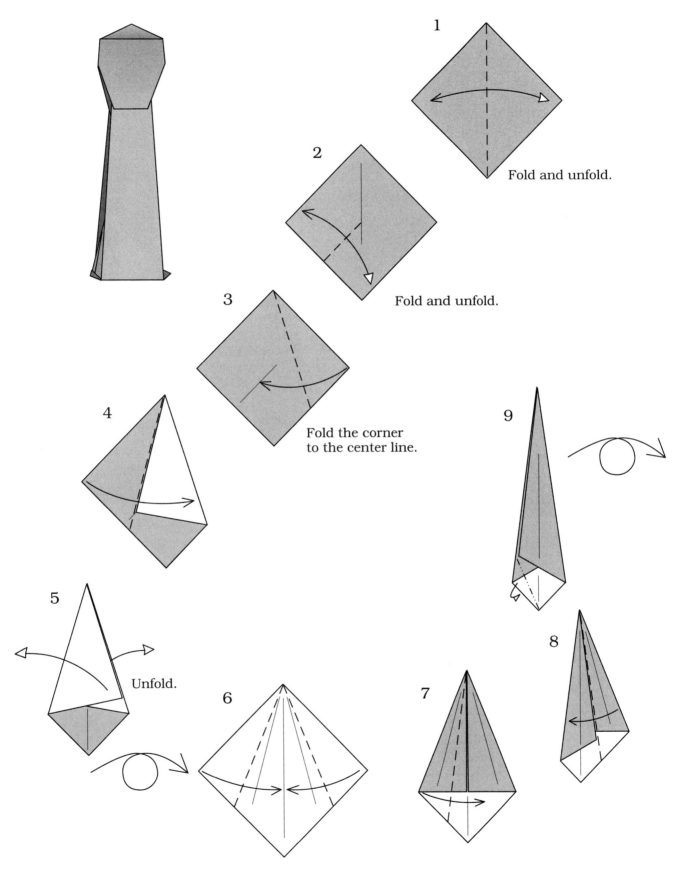

1

Fold and unfold.

2

Fold and unfold.

3

Fold the corner to the center line.

4

5

Unfold.

6

7

8

9

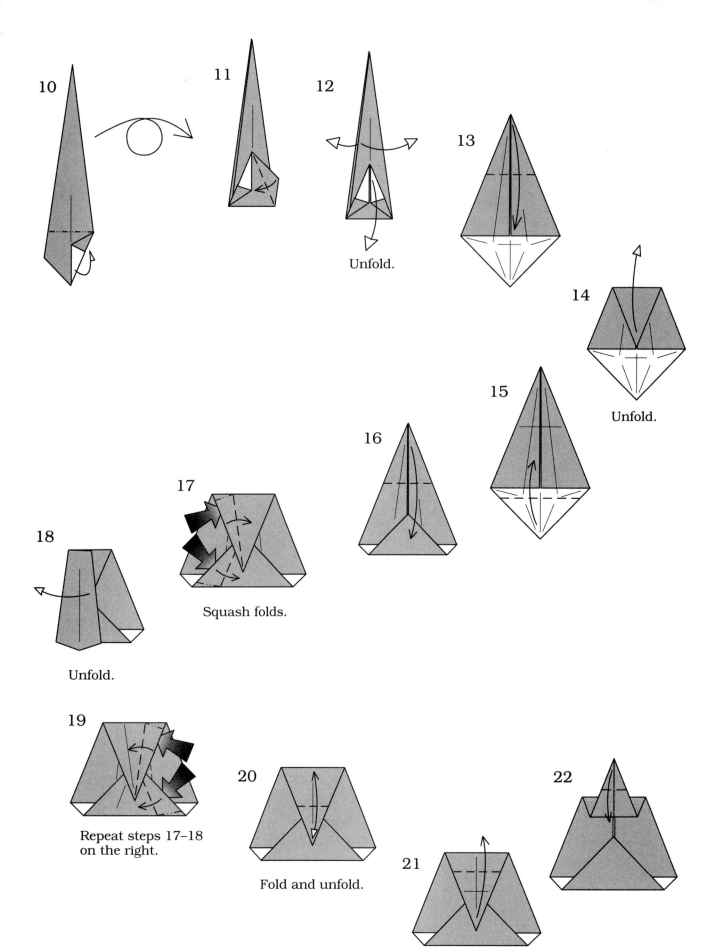

10

11

12

Unfold.

13

14

Unfold.

15

16

17

Squash folds.

18

Unfold.

19

Repeat steps 17–18
on the right.

20

Fold and unfold.

21

22

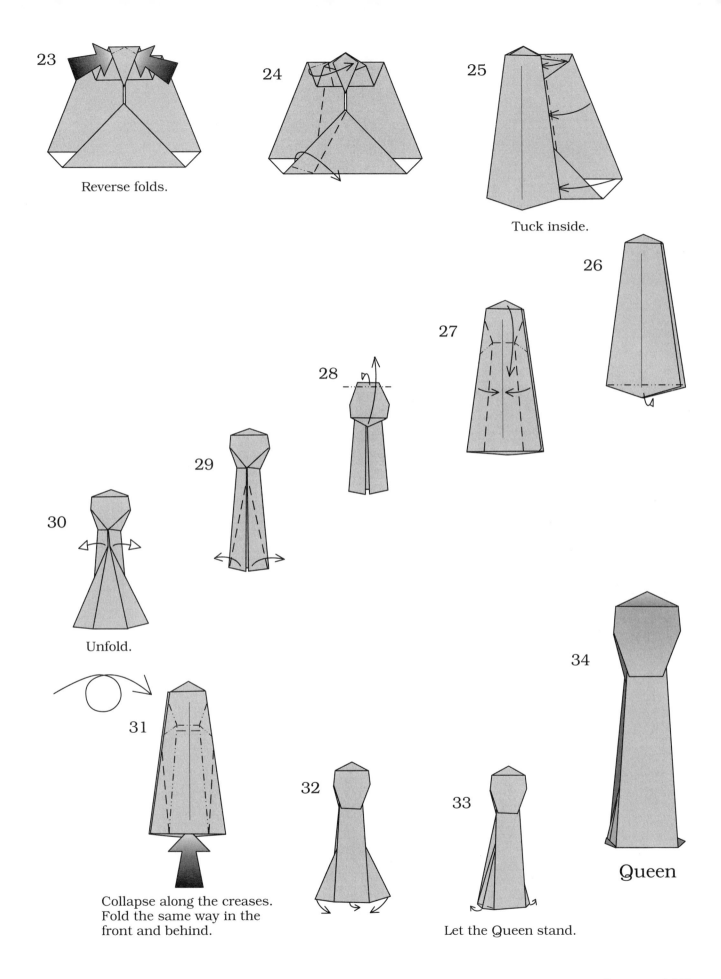

23

Reverse folds.

24

25

Tuck inside.

26

27

28

29

30

Unfold.

31

Collapse along the creases.
Fold the same way in the
front and behind.

32

33

Let the Queen stand.

34

Queen

King

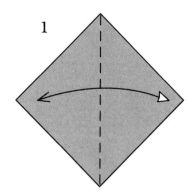

1

Fold and unfold.

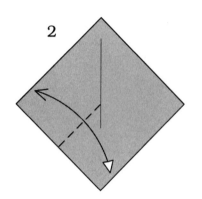

2

Fold and unfold.

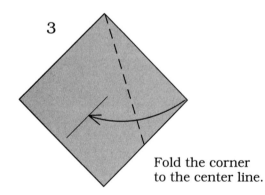

3

Fold the corner
to the center line.

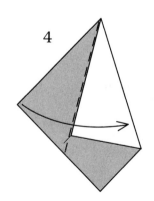

4

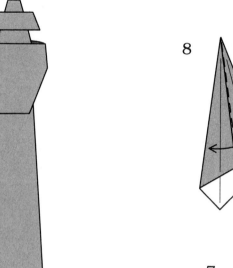

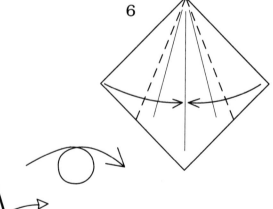

8

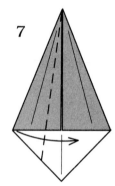

7

6

5

Unfold.

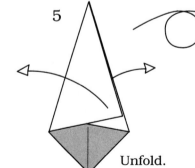

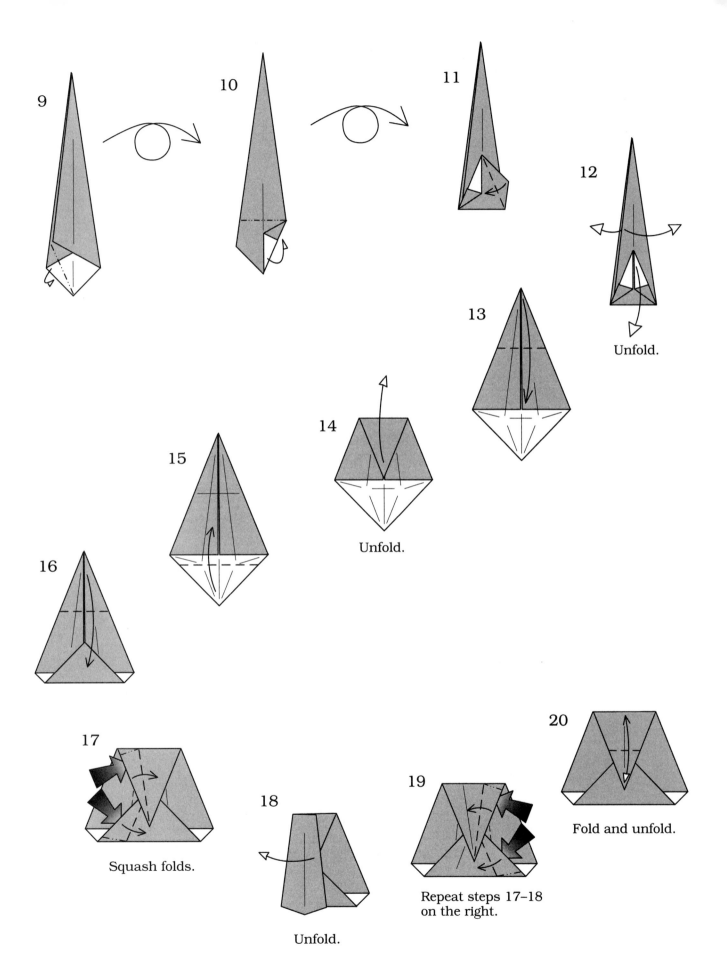

9

10

11

12

Unfold.

13

14

Unfold.

15

16

17

Squash folds.

18

Unfold.

19

Repeat steps 17–18
on the right.

20

Fold and unfold.

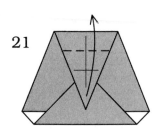

21

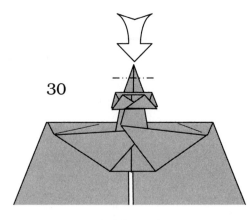

30

Fold inside.

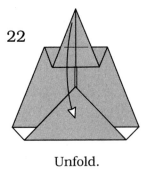

22

Unfold.

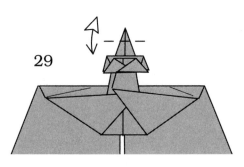

29

Fold and unfold.

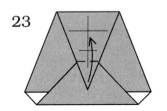

23

Fold up below
the crease line.

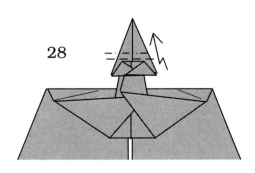

28

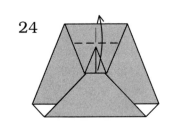

24

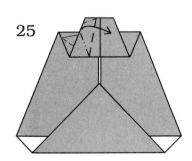

25

Squash-fold.

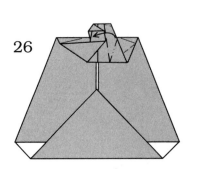

26

Squash-fold.

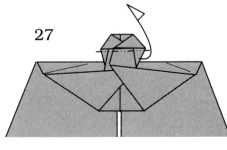

27

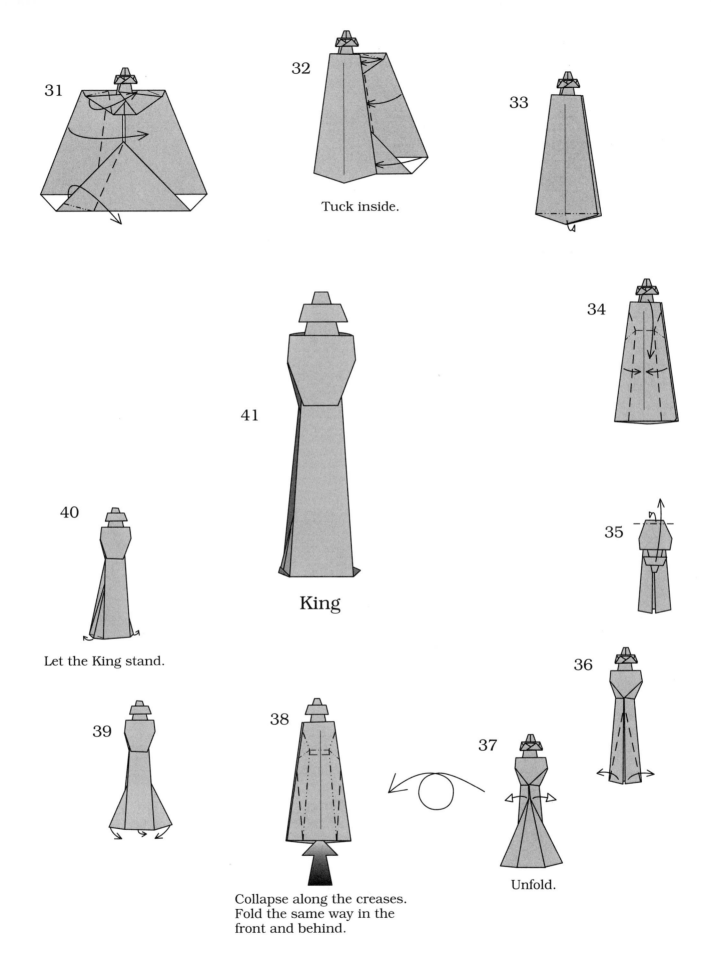

31

32

Tuck inside.

33

34

41

King

35

40

Let the King stand.

36

39

38

37

Collapse along the creases.
Fold the same way in the
front and behind.

Unfold.

Chess Board & Table

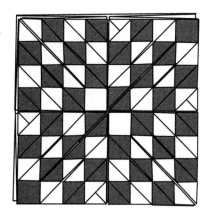

Stage 1: Precreasing

1

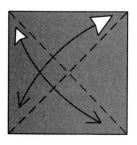

Fold and unfold
along the diagonals.

2

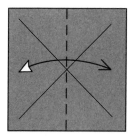

Fold and unfold.

3

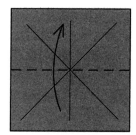

4

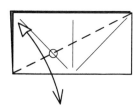

Fold and unfold.
Crease lightly but
sharper by the circle.

5

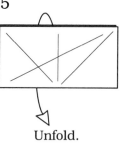

Unfold.

6

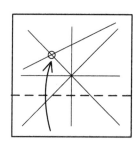

Fold up to the
intersection.

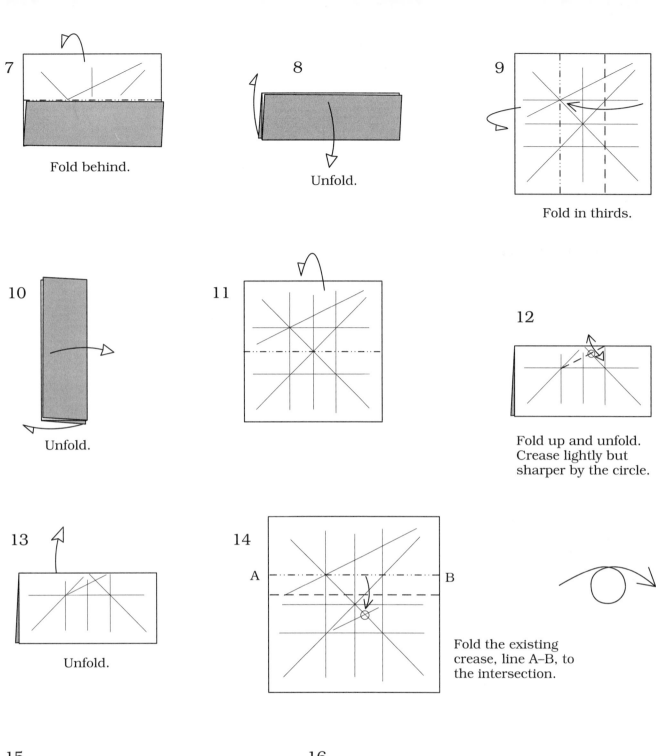

7 Fold behind.

8 Unfold.

9 Fold in thirds.

10 Unfold.

11

12 Fold up and unfold. Crease lightly but sharper by the circle.

13 Unfold.

14 A — B Fold the existing crease, line A–B, to the intersection.

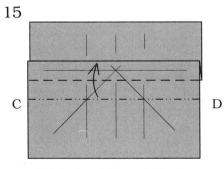

15 C — D Fold along the existing crease, line C–D.

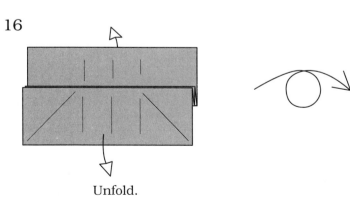

16 Unfold.

17
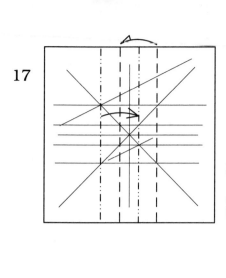

Repeat steps
14–16 in the
opposite direction.
(Fold and unfold.)

18
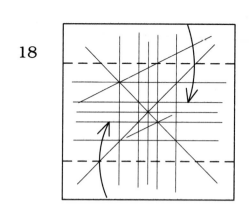

19
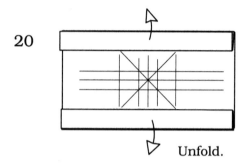

20
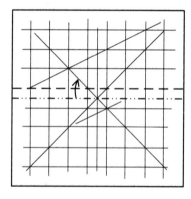

Unfold.

Stage 2: Forming the
Chess Board base.

21
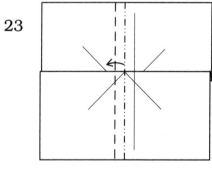

Repeat steps 18–20 in
the opposite direction.

22
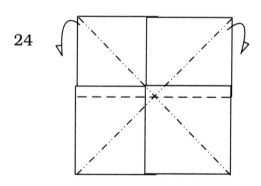

Mountain-fold
along the center.

23

Mountain-fold
along the center.

24

This is similar to folding
the Waterbomb Base.

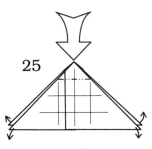

25

Open, as if beginning
to sink. Fold neatly.

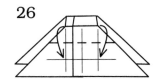

26

Spread-squash-fold.
Fold neatly.

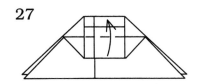

27

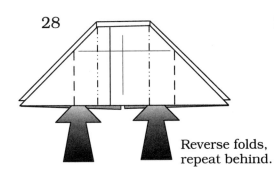

28

Reverse folds,
repeat behind.

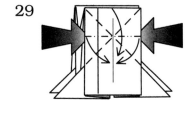

29

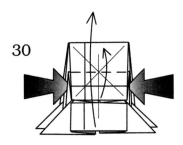

30

Place your fingers inside
the center pockets to
open the model.

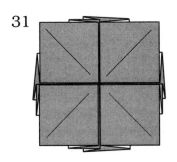

31

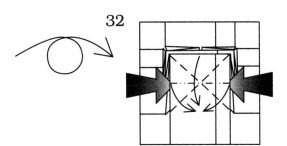

32

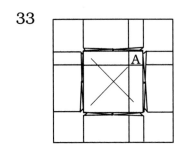

33

Rotate so that the
little square labeled A
is at the lower corner.

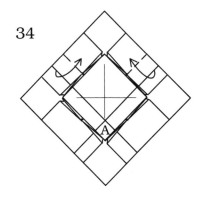

34

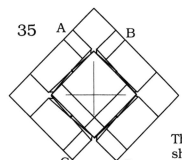

35

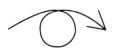

The little rectangles,
shown near the letters,
are at the top and bottom.

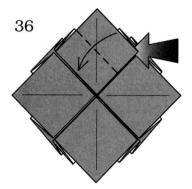

36

Squash-fold.

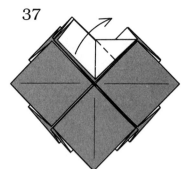

37

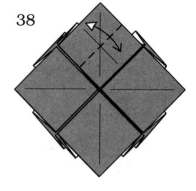

38

Repeat steps 36–37 in
the other direction.

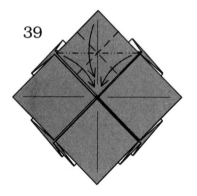

39

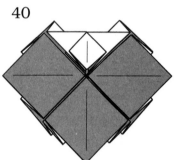

40

Repeat steps 36–39
on the bottom.

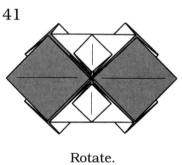

41

Rotate.

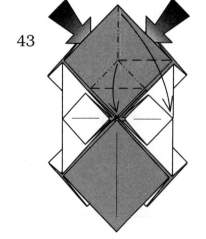

42

Fold and unfold.

43

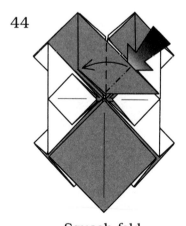

44

Squash-fold.

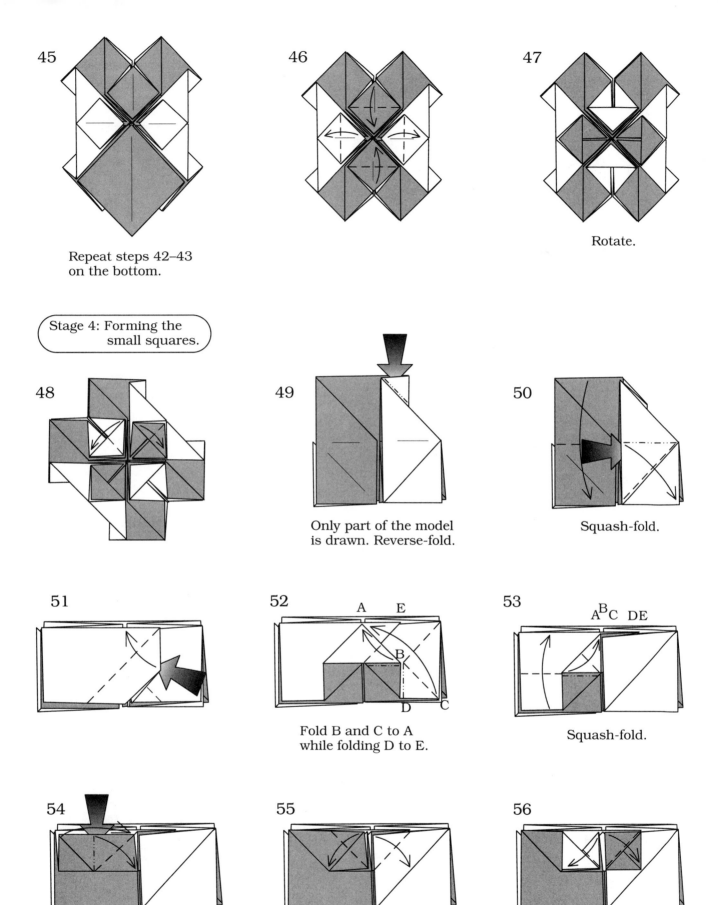

45

Repeat steps 42–43
on the bottom.

46

47

Rotate.

Stage 4: Forming the
small squares.

48

49

Only part of the model
is drawn. Reverse-fold.

50

Squash-fold.

51

52

A   E

B

D   C

Fold B and C to A
while folding D to E.

53

A B C D E

Squash-fold.

54

Squash-fold.

55

56

57

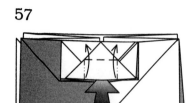

Petal-fold.

58

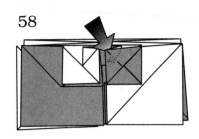

Reverse-fold the inside layer.

59

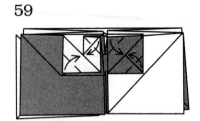

60

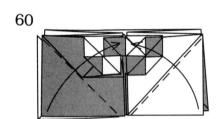

61

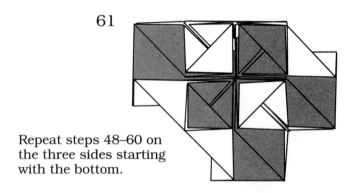

Repeat steps 48–60 on
the three sides starting
with the bottom.

62

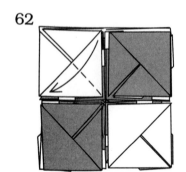

63

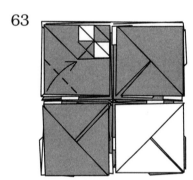

64

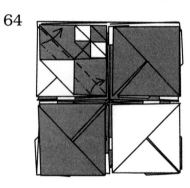

65

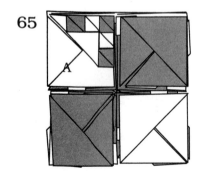

Repeat steps 62–64
on region A.

66

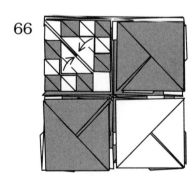

67

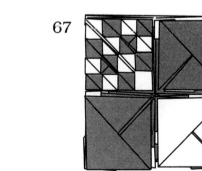

Repeat steps 62–66
on the three sides.

68

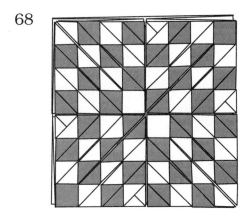

Chess Board

Stage 5: Making legs.

69

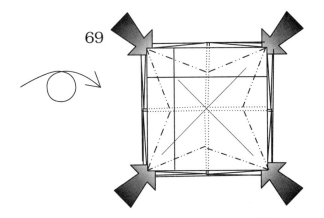

Make eight reverse folds.

70

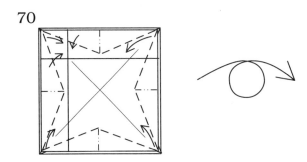

Make the legs three-dimensional.

71

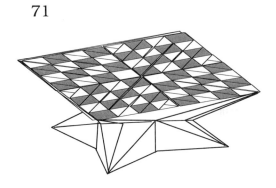

Chess Table

Basic Folds

Rabbit Ear.

To fold a rabbit ear, one corner is folded in half and laid down to a side.

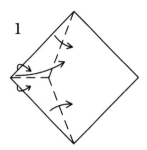

Fold a rabbit ear.

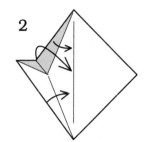

A three-dimensional intermediate step.

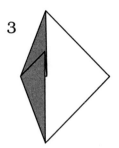

Double Rabbit Ear.

If you were to bend a straw you would be folding the double rabbit ear.

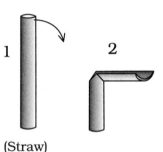

(Straw)

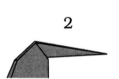

Make a double rabbit ear.

Squash Fold.

In a squash fold, some paper is opened and then made flat. The shaded arrow shows where to place your finger.

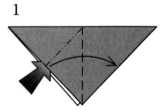

Squash-fold.

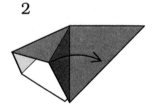

A three-dimensional intermediate step.

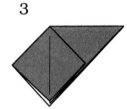

Petal Fold.

In a petal fold, one point is folded up while two opposite sides meet each other.

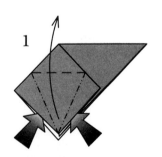

Petal-fold.

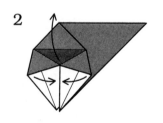

A three-dimensional intermediate step.

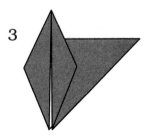

Inside Reverse Fold.

In an inside reverse fold, some paper is folded between layers. Here are two examples.

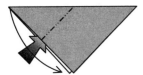 

Reverse-fold.

 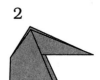

Reverse-fold.

Outside Reverse Fold.

Much of the paper must be unfolded to make an outside reverse fold.

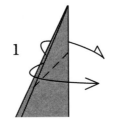 

Outside-reverse-fold.

Crimp Fold.

A crimp fold is a combination of two reverse folds.

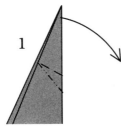 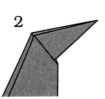

Crimp-fold.

Sink Fold.

In a sink fold, some of the paper without edges is folded inside. To do this fold, much of the model must be unfolded.

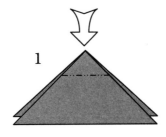 

Sink.

Spread Squash Fold.

A cross between a squash fold and sink fold, some paper in the center is spread apart and then made flat.

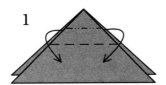 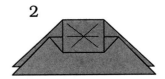

Spread-squash-fold.